Devotions on the Greek New Testament, Volume Two

T0288755

Devotions on the Greek New Testament, Volume Two

52 REFLECTIONS TO INSPIRE & INSTRUCT

Paul N. Jackson, editor

ZONDERVAN

Devotions on the Greek New Testament, Volume Two
Copyright © 2017 by Paul Jackson

This title is also available as a Zondervan ebook.

Requests for information should be addressed to:
Zondervan, 3900 *Sparks Dr. SE, Grand Rapids, Michigan 49546*

ISBN 978-0-310-52935-4

Cover design: *Mark Novelli, www.imagocreative.com*
Cover photo: *Shutterstock; University of Michigan*
Interior design: *Matthew Van Zomeren*

Printed in the United States of America

HB 08.28.2023

Contents

Introduction

Having written one of the devotions for the first volume of this book, *Devotions on the Greek New Testament: 52 Reflections to Inspire & Intruct*, edited by Duvall and Verbrugge, I realized early on the tremendous value of such a practical tool (hereafter *DGNT*). It quickly became a required textbook for my second-semester course of beginning Greek. Since beginning my teaching career at Union University in Jackson, Tennessee in 1993, I constantly desired more practical tools and methods to help my students embrace why I put them through the rigors of what I have dubbed "boot camp Greek." I often wryly told them, "What has been done unto me, shall be done equally unto you," along with, "Repetition is the price of scholarship!" Convincing students who eventually hit what my good friend Bill Mounce calls "the fog" that you can eventually find a practical reason for being there is a tall order. Before *DGNT* appeared in 2012, Mounce's second edition of *Basics of Biblical Greek* appeared in 2003 with each chapter beginning with an exegetical insight related to the grammar lesson that followed. This added feature stirred the pot even more for innovative ways to help students understand why they needed to know this dead language. Thankfully, more commentary series are appearing today that not only deal seriously with the biblical Greek text but also feature substantial sections devoted to practical application. Two marvelous examples are Zondervan's Exegetical Commentary on the New Testament series and Broadman & Holman's Exegetical Guide to the Greek New Testament series. The latter is a continuation of what Murray J. Harris began with *Colossians and Philemon* in 1991 (initially published by Eerdmans). A good number of these have already appeared and continue the excellent work initiated by Harris. The volumes include grammatical analyses, sentence diagramming, and suggested sermon outlines. For years Harris's volume was my favorite commentary.

Using *DGNT* for a few years to help equip my students to write their own short devotion as one of their requirements led me to think about a follow-up volume. I read a number of great reviews of the first one on Amazon.com, but one of them especially jumped out at me: "The only weakness I see with this book is that there is not another one for next year!" So, after receiving the green light from my friend J. Scott Duvall to piggyback on what he originally initiated with the first volume, I approached Verlyn Verbrugge at an ETS meeting about a second volume. His and Scott's enthusiasm moved me to write a proposal that same day! And now here we are with it in front of you. In between these two works, in 2015, *Devotions on the Hebrew Bible: 54 Lessons to Inspire and Instruct* appeared (*DHB*). It is to our dearly missed friend, Verlyn Verbrugge, that *DHB* and *DGNT 2* are both warmly dedicated. One of the brightest highlights of the annual ETS meeting included stopping by the Zondervan booth for a nice chat with Verlyn. He is sorely missed, but his footprint is deep and lasting.

Zondervan wisely thought it important to vary this volume from the first with more international and female scholars. This choice served to give the book a more diverse geographical representation and also provides the church and academia with the keen insights of outstanding scholars we don't hear enough from.

I believe you will enjoy the different sources of significance from which these devotions emerged. It is amazing to see how many times an English translation simply obscures or misses what lies hidden in plain sight in the Greek text. For example, the fine-tuning of an interpretation can result from simply recognizing the gender or number of a relative pronoun. And don't assume a textual variant that a committee chose is necessarily the last word on what could be a plausible meaning in an otherwise disfavored text, or the

180-degree difference the discovery of an older or overlooked textual variant can make in how one's theology is directed. Word choice, word order, word nuance, word tense or case, word frequency, and word play all come under consideration throughout these devotions. We are reminded also of the importance of simple prepositions, connectives, and particles that are sandwiched between the verbs, nouns, participles, infinitives, adverbs, and adjectives.

I want to thank all of the authors for their insightful contributions. Through them I have come to the happy realization how many excellent Greek scholars we have ministering in the church and academia in so many different places. Thanks also to two ace, Zondervan biblical-languages and reference-tools editors, Nancy Erickson and Chris Beetham, for their professional editing, encouragement, and friendship during the making of this book. I thank Union University, my teaching post for nearly a quarter of a century, and President Samuel "Dub" Oliver, Provost C. Ben Mitchell, and Dean Nathan Finn for their part in approving my time away. And I thank the loving and generous congregation I pastor known as the Westside Baptist Church in Halls, Tennessee for allowing me time away from my pastoral duties to fulfill this calling. In my absence, they had the rich blessing of hearing Dub Oliver, Ben Mitchell, and Harry Lee Poe preach and teach. I thank them also for pulling extra duty on my behalf.

As I write this introduction, I am sitting in my temporary office at the *Centro Para O Desenvolvimento De Liderança* (Center for Leadership Development) in Matola, Mozambique. I want to thank its founder, Dr. Isaias Uaene, for the invitation to spend my research leave teaching Greek. I thank above all my loving wife Janet, who along with Amber Woodard, our girls' nanny, are taking care of our five girls: Hailey, Aniya, Madison, Adrianna, and Maleigha. They have all sacrificed much to adjust to an extremely difficult but vastly rewarding change of culture for six months of our lives while I wrote, taught, and preached.

Paul N. Jackson

Abbreviations

AB   Anchor Bible

BDAG   Danker, Frederick W., Walter Bauer, William F. Arndt, and F. W. Gingrich. *Greek-English Lexicon of the New Testament and Other Early Christian Literature.* 3rd ed. Chicago: University of Chicago Press, 2000.

BECNT   Baker Exegetical Commentary on the New Testament

BibInt   Biblical Interpretation Series

CEB   Common English Bible

DGNT   *Devotions on the Greek New Testament.* Grand Rapids: Zondervan, 2012.

ESV   English Standard Version

GNB   Good News Bible (= Today's English Version)

HCSB   Holman Christian Standard Bible

ICC   International Critical Commentary

JBL   *Journal of Biblical Literature*

KJV   King James Version

L&N   Louw, Johannes P., and Eugene A. Nida, eds. *Greek-English Lexicon of the New Testament: Based on Semantic Domains.* 2nd ed. New York: United Bible Societies, 1989.

LCL   Loeb Classical Library

LSJ   Liddell, Henry George, Robert Scott, Henry Stuart Jones. *A Greek-English Lexicon.* 9th ed. Oxford: Clarendon, 1996.

LXX   Septuagint (the Greek Old Testament)

MIT   MacDonald Idiomatic Translation

MM   Moulton, James H., and George Milligan. *The Vocabulary of the Greek Testament.* London: Hodder and Stoughton, 1930.

MT   Masoretic Text

NA²⁷   *Novum Testamentum Graece,* Nestle-Aland, 27th ed.

NA²⁸   *Novum Testamentum Graece,* Nestle-Aland, 28th ed.

NAB   New American Bible

NASB   New American Standard Bible, 1995 edition

NEB   New English Bible

NET   New English Translation

NIV   New International Version, 2011 edition

NJB   New Jerusalem Bible

NLT   New Living Translation

NRSV   New Revised Standard Version

pl.   plural

RSV   Revised Standard Version

RV   Revised Version

sg.   singular

SBLGNT   The Greek New Testament: SBL Edition

TEV   Today's English Version (= Good News Bible)

UBS⁵   *The Greek New Testament,* United Bible Societies, 5th ed.

WBC   Word Biblical Commentary

WH   Westcott-Hort

To Whose Family Line Does Jesus Belong?

MATTHEW 1:16

Ἰακὼβ δὲ ἐγέννησεν τὸν Ἰωσὴφ τὸν ἄνδρα Μαρίας, ἐξ ἧς ἐγεννήθη Ἰησοῦς ὁ λεγόμενος Χριστός.

Matthew begins his Gospel with an extensive genealogy that runs from Abraham to Jesus through Joseph (1:1–16). Yet Matthew breaks his pattern of "X was the father of Y" just as he gets to Joseph. Instead, he describes Joseph as "the husband of Mary, from whom [ἐξ ἧς] was born Jesus" (v. 16). While in English this translation can imply that Jesus is born from both Mary and Joseph, in the Greek the author emphasizes Mary's parentage, breaking from his established genealogical pattern.

In Greek, relative pronouns, like the one in Matthew 1:16 ("from *whom*"), always possess gender, number, and case. Relative pronouns in English, on the other hand, are distinguished from each other only by case ("who," "whom"). Matthew uses the relative pronoun ἧς, which is a feminine, singular, genitive pronoun. If he had wanted to indicate that Jesus came from both Joseph and Mary, he would have used a plural masculine form (ὧν). By using a feminine, singular relative pronoun, Matthew emphasizes that Jesus is the offspring of Mary. He will reaffirm that something special is going on in 1:20 (Jesus is conceived "from the Holy Spirit"). This is the conundrum of the genealogy: How does Jesus come from Joseph's lineage if he is born from Mary and not Joseph?

Matthew does not keep us in suspense for long. He unravels the puzzle in 1:18–25 by emphasizing in narrative fashion that Joseph adopts Jesus into his family and so into his family line. In that social context, it was the father's prerogative to name his children (cf. Luke 1:59–63). By naming Jesus, Joseph effectively adopts him as his own.

Matthew twice mentions the naming of Jesus by Joseph, once in the angel's instructions to Joseph (1:21) and once at the end of the story—its climax—as Joseph obeys the Lord's angel and names (adopts) Jesus (v. 25). Yet Matthew not only underscores this naming of Jesus but also uses Jesus's name as an *inclusio* or bookend for all of verses 18–25, something that can be seen clearly only in the Greek text. Jesus's name is the first word of this passage as well as its last. Matthew 1:18 begins Τοῦ δὲ Ἰησοῦ, with the Greek article accompanying Jesus's name. (Names in Greek often have articles, although because English does not have this convention we cannot render it with an English article.) And the very last word of Matthew 1:25 is Ἰησοῦν. Jesus is named by Joseph, and he is named "Jesus," which reflects the Hebrew *yeshua/yehoshua* meaning "Yahweh saves." Matthew points this out in 1:21: "He will save [σώσει] his people from their sins." Finally, Matthew further accents the importance of naming in 1:18–25 by providing his own name for Jesus, one derived from the Jewish Scriptures. Jesus will be called "'Immanuel,' which means 'God with us'" (1:23, quoting Isa 7:14).

Matthew begins his Gospel with a genealogy—concluding with a conundrum—for good reason. First, he wants to emphasize that Jesus comes from the line of David through Joseph, who is himself a "son of David" (1:20). Jesus is the royal Messiah-King, who will establish God's kingdom in this world. Second, Matthew presses his readers to recognize Jesus as Savior. Jesus will save his people, Israel, from sin and death; and, by doing so, he will bring salvation to all peoples (28:19). Finally, Matthew is supremely interested in revealing that Jesus is "Immanuel, God with us" (1:23; μεθ' ἡμῶν). To ensure that we understand, Matthew concludes his Gospel with these words of assurance from Jesus himself: "I am with you (μεθ' ὑμῶν) always, even to the end of the age" (28:20). He is Immanuel from beginning to end, and everywhere in between.

Jeannine K. Brown

ἁγιασθήτω τὸ ὄνομά σου,
ἐλθέτω ἡ βασιλεία σου,
γενηθήτω τὸ θέλημά σου

Though the Lord's Prayer is not a script for us to follow, it is a model: it should *inform* our prayers. Focusing on its first half, I want to look at how the Greek text illuminates such reflection.

The Lord's Prayer is a part of the Sermon on the Mount. Here Jesus teaches principles that characterize the radical kingdom he announces and the attitudes and behavior that characterize those who participate in it.

And so, Jesus teaches a kingdom prayer. He establishes the standards of good practice for his followers first through negative examples that teach them how they should *not* pray (vv. 5–8), and, second, through a model prayer that teaches them how they *should* pray (vv. 9–13; "*You*, then, make it your habit to pray like this," οὕτως οὖν προσεύχεσθε ὑμεῖς; v. 9). The context suggests that the imperative in v. 9 is best taken as a customary present, expressing a habitual action. Contrary to those whose prayers are habitually self-promoting, those whose prayers follow Jesus's model cultivate a different habit.

This kingdom prayer has six petitions, grouped in two sets of three. The first set presents requests about God: three clauses, each with a third-person, aorist imperative verb, followed by a noun modified by a second-person possessive pronoun (vv. 9–10). The imperative is a natural choice in prayer, because it is the verbal form normally used when someone of lower status communicates to a superior.[1] The second set of petitions presents requests about human needs (vv. 11–13). Each of these petitions contains a first-person, plural pronoun, and the second and third petitions are connected to the previous one by καί ("and") to form one long sentence.

I will focus on the first set of petitions, those about God (vv. 9–10). As mentioned above, these petitions have the same form, rendered literally as:

> May your name be honored,
> May your kingdom/reign come,
> May your will be done,
>   as [it is done] in heaven, also [may it be done]
>   on the earth.

Our English translations may lead us to think that the first petition is a statement or declaration (i.e., "hallowed be your name" = "your name is holy"). We have seen that the Greek verb, however, is not an indicative but an imperative that expresses a petition. It is a request to God that his name be treated as holy because at the present time it is not always so. Essentially this is a plea for the coming of God's kingdom, which Jesus says has drawn near (4:17). The second request articulates this plea: "May your kingdom come!"

The third request extends the plea for God's kingdom to come in its fullness. Its word order in the Greek is illuminating. The emphasis is on the first clause, "as in heaven." God's will *is* done in heaven in a way not yet done on earth. The point is not simply to pray that God accomplish his will, but that God accomplish it on earth *as it is [already done in heaven].*

---

1. See Daniel B. Wallace, *Greek Grammar Beyond the Basics* (Grand Rapids: Zondervan, 1996), 488.

Through repetition and variation, the first three petitions ask God to realize his kingdom in all its fullness. Yet it is not a passive prayer. It is not a request that God act while human beings wait and watch. This kingdom prayer orients Jesus's followers to the present revelation of God's future reign. As a result, we may live in this kingdom by promoting God's person, will, and ways rather than our own.

Elizabeth E. Shively

When a Sinner Refuses to Listen

MATTHEW 18:17

ἐὰν δὲ παρακούσῃ αὐτῶν, εἰπὲ τῇ ἐκκλησίᾳ· ἐὰν δὲ καὶ τῆς ἐκκλησίας παρακούσῃ, ἔστω σοι ὥσπερ ὁ ἐθνικὸς καὶ ὁ τελώνης.

Pronouns matter, but it is sometimes difficult to see how in modern English. For example, we have only one form of the second-person pronoun, whether singular or plural: you. Consequently, when we read verses in the Bible that address "you," we can't tell if the matter pertains to an individual "you" or the group "you" (known in the South as "y'all"). The difference can be crucial, especially when we consider passages like Matthew 18:17. Some think that Jesus taught the church to excommunicate unrepentant sinners. And, when we read his instructions in English, it is easy to see why. Jesus appears to give a four-step procedure that leads to the excommunication of an unrepentant sinner (Matt 18:15–17). Step one: a disciple confronts another disciple who is sinning (obviously, a sin that is known to both of them). If the disciple "listens to him" (a vague response that could mean several things—from a respectful hearing to repentance), he or she has regained that disciple. If the sinner refuses to listen (whatever that means), then proceed to step two: bring in one or two more "witnesses" to rebuke the sinner. If the sinner refuses to listen to them, then move on to step three: take the matter before the church. Finally, if the sinner still refuses to listen to them, go to step four: "Let him be *to you* as a gentile and a tax collector" (v. 17). Following the progression (from individual confrontation to group involvement), it sounds as if Jesus were giving instructions to the church to excommunicate an unrepentant sinner, reading "to you" in this case as a plural pronoun. But for those of us who read Greek, we know that's *not* what Jesus was teaching here. The second-person pronoun of step four is *singular*: ἔστω σοι ὥσπερ ὁ ἐθνικὸς καὶ ὁ τελώνης. According to Matthew's Greek translation of Jesus's words (whether Aramaic or Hebrew), Jesus wasn't giving advice to the church, instructing the assembly to kick out the rebel. Rather, *throughout this passage* Jesus was giving advice to one individual about another individual. In other words, Jesus didn't teach the entire church to shun the unrepentant sinner. Rather, he told the concerned disciple to treat the disciple who refused to listen like a "gentile and a tax collector." But what does that mean?

We could answer the question with a question: How did Jesus treat gentiles and tax collectors? Both groups were marginalized as outsiders in Jewish society. Bringing the kingdom of heaven to earth, Jesus treated outsiders like insiders, willing to go to the house of a Roman soldier and heal his slave or to eat with a bunch of tax collectors and "sinners" (8:5–7; 9:10). Despite the Pharisees' objection, Jesus ate with "sick" sinners because they needed a physician (9:11–12). Indeed, the Pharisees needed to learn a lesson from Hosea. According to the prophet, God wants mercy more than sacrifice (v. 13, quoting Hos 6:6). Therefore, when it comes to notorious sinners who refuse to listen to righteous people, the way of Jesus was to show them mercy. Besides, Jesus's instruction concerning how to treat sinners who refuse to listen comes immediately after his teaching about recovering lost sheep—those who wander from the fold of God (Matt 18:12–14). In fact, he gave similar instruction to the twelve when he sent them out to recover "the lost sheep of Israel" (10:6). To restore the "harassed and helpless, like sheep without a shepherd" (9:36 NRSV), Jesus sent his disciples to heal the sick—just like the Roman centurion's slave—and proclaim that the kingdom of heaven "has come near," going home with those who invite them to their table (10:6–13)—even lost sheep like tax collectors and sinners.

Rodney Reeves

Why Jesus Has Come

MARK 1:23–26

²⁴ Τί ἡμῖν καὶ σοί, Ἰησοῦ Ναζαρηνέ; ἦλθες ἀπολέσαι ἡμᾶς; οἶδά σε τίς εἶ, ὁ ἅγιος τοῦ θεοῦ.

A discussion of singular and plural nouns and verbs might seem like recourse to basic Greek. But attention to elementary grammar often supplies exegetical rewards, and, indeed, overlooking it may result in missing the gist of a passage. Mark 1:23–26 is a case in point. These verses fit into the story of Jesus's first public appearance in Mark's Gospel (vv. 21–28). Jesus teaches in the Capernaum synagogue and performs his first exorcism there when an unclean spirit that possesses a man engages him in a verbal battle. Jesus answers the possessed man's words with a command to "be silent and come out of him," showing that the unclean spirit, rather than the man, is the prime agent in the skirmish. Mark focuses on the unclean spirit's agency by using singular forms throughout vv. 23–26:

> A man with an unclean spirit [ἐν πνεύματι ἀκαθάρτῳ, sg. noun] was in the synagogue, and he cried out [ἀνέκραξεν, sg. verb], "I know [οἶδα, sg. verb] who you are. . . ." Jesus answered him [αὐτῷ, sg. pronoun], "Be silent [Φιμώθητι, sg. verb] and come out [ἔξελθε, sg. verb]." The unclean spirit [τὸ πνεῦμα τὸ ἀκάθαρτον, sg. noun] came out [ἐξῆλθεν, sg. verb], after convulsing [σπαράξαν, sg. participle] him and crying out [φωνῆσαν, sg. participle].

Yet verse 24 provides two exceptions to this string of singular forms. The unclean spirit asks, "What have you to do with

26

us [ἡμῖν, pl. pronoun]? Have you come to destroy *us* [ἡμᾶς, pl. pronoun]?" The two plural pronouns contrast starkly with the singular verb οἶδα (v. 24) and with all the other singular forms in the passage.

Without a careful look at these plural pronouns within the context of the string of singular forms, we might conclude that they signal that a host of demons possesses this man, similar to what we find in the Gerasene demoniac story (5:1–20). Yet there Mark uses plural forms to refer to the unclean spirits, but only after he introduces the demons as a legion. However, here in 1:23–26 the singular forms dominate. *One* unclean spirit possesses the man, not a legion. The implication is that the unclean spirit acts as a spokesperson for the rest of the demon horde when the spirit remarks, "What have you to do with *us* [ἡμῖν, pl. pronoun], Jesus of Nazareth? Have you come to destroy *us* [ἡμᾶς, pl. pronoun]? *I know* [οἶδα, sg.] who you are, the holy one of God." Jesus's rebuke, "Be silent [sg.], and come out [sg.] of him!" (v. 25) functions as an answer to the unclean spirit's question by indicating that he has indeed come to destroy the demonic realm.

This simple grammatical point underscores the programmatic significance of the Capernaum synagogue account for Mark's Gospel. According to Mark, Jesus begins his public ministry at the Capernaum synagogue just after the wilderness conflict with Satan and his announcement of the kingdom of God. The exorcism that accompanies Jesus's teaching there both confirms his authority and demonstrates a key purpose of his mission—the defeat of Satan's power. The rest of the Gospel develops this purpose. According to Mark, Jesus's ministry, death, and resurrection bring a decisive end to Satan's pernicious hold upon humanity and the world. This is why he has come.

Elizabeth E. Shively

Stay Salty, My Friends

MARK 9:42–50

⁴² καὶ ὃς ἂν σκανδαλίσῃ → ἕνα τῶν μικρῶν τούτων
                                 τῶν πιστευόντων [εἰς ἐμέ],
(1) καλόν ἐστιν αὐτῷ μᾶλλον
        εἰ περίκειται μύλος ὀνικὸς
                περὶ τὸν τράχηλον αὐτοῦ
            καὶ
            βέβληται
                εἰς τὴν θάλασσαν.
⁴³   καὶ
        ἐὰν σκανδαλίζῃ → σε ἡ χείρ σου,
ἀπόκοψον → αὐτήν·
(2) καλόν ἐστίν σε κυλλὸν εἰσελθεῖν
                                εἰς τὴν ζωὴν
                                ἢ
        (σε).... ἀπελθεῖν
                    ^ἔχοντα → τὰς δύο χεῖρας...
                    εἰς τὴν γέενναν,
                    εἰς τὸ πῦρ τὸ ἄσβεστον.
⁴⁵   καὶ
        ἐὰν ὁ πούς σου σκανδαλίζῃ σε,
ἀπόκοψον → αὐτόν·
(3) καλόν ἐστίν σε εἰσελθεῖν χωλὸν
                εἰς τὴν ζωὴν
                ἢ
                ἔχοντα→τοὺς δύο πόδας...
        (σε)...βληθῆναι
                εἰς τὴν γέενναν.

28

47   καὶ

     ἐὰν ὁ ὀφθαλμός σου σκανδαλίζῃ → σε,

ἔκβαλε → αὐτόν·

           ^μονόφθαλμον

(4) καλόν σέ ἐστιν …… εἰσελθεῖν

           εἰς τὴν βασιλείαν τοῦ θεοῦ

             ἢ

         ^ἔχοντα → δύο ὀφθαλμοὺς

    (σε)…..βληθῆναι

           εἰς τὴν γέενναν,

48   ὅπου ὁ σκώληξ αὐτῶν οὐ τελευτᾷ

                         καὶ

                     τὸ πῦρ οὐ σβέννυται·

^γὰρ

49 πᾶς … …. ἁλισθήσεται.

          ^^πυρὶ

(5) 50 Καλὸν τὸ ἅλας·

    ^δὲ

         ἐὰν …. τὸ ἅλας ἄναλον γένηται,

         ἐν τίνι

         ἀρτύσετε → ^αὐτὸ

ἔχετε …. → ἅλα,

   ^ἐν ἑαυτοῖς

    καὶ

εἰρηνεύετε

    ἐν ἀλλήλοις.

While parables served as Jesus's most popular method of teaching, he also used hyperbole, repetition, chiasm, irony, and wordplay. Employing overstatement laced with wry puns has the power to plant ideas not easily uprooted. Such is the case with a series of aphorisms Jesus uttered in Mark 9:42–50 about the scandal of sin. In v. 42 Jesus voices his greatest concern first—causing the downfall of even "one of these little ones" (ἑνὰ τῶν μικρῶν τούτων). The verb σκανδαλίζω appears four times in vv. 42–47, translated as "cause the downfall" (HCSB), "causes to sin" (RSV), or "causes to stumble" (NIV). The word apparently at times served as a hunting term ("to snare" or "trap").[1] So, who are these endangered "little ones"? Reaching back to v. 33 provides an answer—children. The context, however, must also include new disciples who, along with children, would be especially susceptible to spiritual failure. For ensnaring such a person, Jesus says that it is "better" (καλόν) to have a huge millstone draped around one's "neck" (τράχηλον) and then cast into the sea to drown. He doesn't say immediately what is worse than this, but it must be eventually finding oneself in the fires of Gehenna (γέεννα; vv. 43, 45, and 47). Because of the potential danger of sowing seeds of disaster in unseasoned Christians, we must regard this warning with the highest measure of caution. In this opening example, the first of five wordplays (καλόν/τράχηλον—better/ neck) and/or rhymes appears. The first four include the hyperboles of drowning by millstone and the violent removal of body parts. The five wordplay pairs are listed in the chart below. Notice that σκανδαλίζω, the "trigger verb," is missing from the fifth pair, as the last pairing appears after the γάρ in verse 49 where Jesus explains how to maximize protection against the crippling potential of tests and temptations that are certain to come.

In turn, if someone's hand (v. 43), foot (v. 45), or eye (v. 47) ensnares them, they are exhorted to chop it off or rip it out! Referring to these body parts could be metonymy, but it's most likely the Old Testament idea that the hand and eye are the instruments used to sin, and the feet are used to take us where we are going to commit it (see Job 31:1–12 and Ps 28:4).[2] Are these measures to

---

1. See LSJ 1064 and MM 576.
2. Mark Strauss, *Mark*, Zondervan Exegetical Commentary on the New Testament (Zondervan, 2014), 414.

be taken literally as Origen of Alexandria did, or is Jesus warning us of something far worse in a graphic, poetic manner? Here is a test. The next time you can, scan a large gathering of Christians and notice the absence of great numbers of eye patches, crutches, and wheelchairs. So, what's more likely—that most of us don't take these sayings literally or that we rarely sin? Surely, because unchecked sin can utterly devastate our lives, the measures we take to "chop it off" (ἀπόκοψον) or "rip it out" (ἔκβαλε) should be as noticeable and lifesaving as amputation!

It is striking to see that in numbers 1 through 3 above the three pairs of words καλόν/τράχηλον (v. 42), καλόν/κυλλόν (v. 43), and καλόν/χωλόν (v. 45) are mostly homonymous. The consonantal sounds of κ, λ, and ν in καλόν are paired each time with those of χ, λ, and ν in τράχηλον, κ, λλ, and ν in κυλλόν, and χ, λ, and ν in χωλόν respectively. Each pair occurs in a main clause and is linked with referents that create irony. How can drowning or losing body parts be καλός? That's the irony! The framing of these three pairs cause the hearer to think of each pair as one in the same. Yahweh did a similar thing to Jeremiah with the Hebrew words for "almond tree" (shaqed) and "to watch" (shoqed) (Jer 1:11–12). When Jeremiah sees the shaqed, he will know that God is shoqed! You see? Any language will do. When we come to the fourth pair, the homonymy softens to a rhyme, καλόν/μονόφθαλμον, but we still hear "λον-μον-μον" and by this time in the lesson it still delivers the same ironic punch. So hyperbole, chiasm, ironic wordplay, the fourfold repetition of σκανδαλίζω, and the shuddering picture of hellfire all drive home the urgency of Jesus's warnings and the reality of divine judgment. Yet there is a positive twist in the conclusion.

The explanatory γάρ in v. 49 introduces a bridging frame that connects *fire* and *salt*: πᾶς γὰρ πυρὶ ἁλισθήσεται ("for everyone will be salted with fire"). This is a tough clause to interpret, but taking this context into account, it probably is connected to the rigorous demands of discipleship. And if the picture of salt purifying a sacrifice referred to in Leviticus 2:13 is in the background, then it makes sense; further, the idea is also akin to Paul's imperative in Romans 12:1 to "present your bodies as living sacrifices" at the outset of the practical application section of that letter.[3] The final καλόν appearing in v. 50 declares that salt is good unless it becomes ἄναλον. This fifth and final pairing is what we want to avoid—"to become saltless" (i.e., to lose our witness; see Matt 5:13–15). Also, notice while ἄναλον still rhymes with καλόν, connecting it with the previous four in sound, it is now disconnected from καλόν grammatically. Every καλόν before the γάρ is best translated "better," but καλόν is translated "good" after it, functioning now as the predicate nominative of τὸ ἅλας. This change in construction shifts our focus to what is truly good: salt! So, better the salty fires of testing now by addressing sin in our lives with surgical-like precision than ending up in Gehenna fully intact forever! The twin imperatives in v. 50 (ἔχετε ἐν ἑαυτοῖς ἅλα; καὶ εἰρηνεύετε ἐν ἀλλήλοις) are intended to emphasize the measures of prevention, demonstrating that genuine discipleship is presently costly but eternally rewarding.[4] So, stay salty, my friends, and enjoy the fruit of peace that accountable discipleship can produce, even if you arrive in heaven figuratively missing some body parts!

Paul N. Jackson

---

3. Some Western texts (D it) contain a scribal attempt to solve the mystery by replacing πυρί with θυσία ἁλί (a sacrifice offered with salt) to connect it verbally to Lev 2:13.
4. See also 1 Cor 3:13–15.

Jesus Echoes Prophetic, Symbolic Actions

MARK 11:17

καὶ ἐδίδασκεν καὶ ἔλεγεν αὐτοῖς, Οὐ γέγραπται ὅτι Ὁ οἶκός μου οἶκος προσευχῆς κληθήσεται πᾶσιν τοῖς ἔθνεσιν; ὑμεῖς δὲ πεποιήκατε αὐτὸν σπήλαιον λῃστῶν.

Prophetic symbolic actions intensified the ministries of Ezekiel, Jeremiah, and Isaiah. Their arresting, vivid dramatizations of the word of God created lasting impressions. In Mark 11 Jesus dismantles an entire system with prophetic symbolic action of his own. When he overturns the tables in the temple, he acts out and foreshadows its destruction. His scathing remarks that follow sealed his fate and inaugurated his death sentence.

Jesus's masterful conflation of Isaiah 56:7 and Jeremiah 7:11 packs a powerful punch against the temple leadership and system. These two prophetic texts require careful attention. The first is typically understood as a message to the postexilic community wrought with chaos, confusion, and conflict between the priestly and prophetic groups. Isaiah 56 is a call to justice and righteousness marked by inclusive worship with the foreigner, the eunuch, and the outcasts of Israel who keep the covenant. Those once excluded by Deuteronomic law (Deut 23:1–2) are now welcomed, and Isaiah celebrates and justifies this covenant identity because "my house shall be called a house of prayer for all peoples" (Isa 56:7). The Septuagint equivalent for "peoples" is typically λαός,

33

but here in Isaiah ἔθνος is chosen. The term ἔθνος designates nations in general and in particular those gentile nations that are distinct from the Jews.

The second text is part of Jeremiah's caustic temple sermon wherein the prophet condemns the temple cult and predicts its fall (Jer 7:1–8:3). The covenant is corrupted, and the people trust lies (7:4, 8–10). After calling for justice and righteousness (vv. 5–7), the Lord in v. 11 asks through Jeremiah, "Has this house, which is called by my name, become a den of robbers in your eyes?" Without missing a beat, the response is given: "'I, even I, have seen it,' says the Lord." Jeremiah recalls the destruction of Shiloh as a foreshadowing of the destruction of Judah and her temple (vv. 12–14). Jeremiah's "den of robbers" is understood as a refuge for persons of violence; it is the place where thugs, who have committed such terrible acts against the covenant people of God, hide out (v. 9). His language declares the moral and ethical bankruptcy of the temple worshippers, and his words are so toxic that the priests, false prophets, and all the people seize him, demanding his death (26:8).

Both Isaiah 56 and Jeremiah 7 subvert the tradition of the holiness of Zion, which put forward the temple, Zion, and Jerusalem as asylums of divine security and privilege. Their predictions about inclusive worship and the destruction of the temple undermine one of the most sacred and widely held beliefs of ancient Israel.

In Mark's Gospel at 11:17, Jesus is speaking to an audience that knows this history. The phrase οὐ γέγραπται, with the perfect passive indicative of the verb γράφω, clarifies the culmination and completion of the prophetic writings with which the audience is well acquainted. Jesus is stating the obvious, and by using the particle of negation, οὐ, he asks a direct question with the expectation of an affirmative answer. The audience that knew these writings and their corresponding contexts felt Jesus's words with their full force. No doubt, some were in shock that Jesus was quoting such dangerous and volatile texts from Isaiah and Jeremiah. It is, therefore, no surprise that the scribes and chief priests respond to Jesus's disruption by seeking to destroy him (v. 18). Such relevant contemporizing of the prophetic texts bears witness to the dynamic and living quality of the words of God as first uttered as many as eight centuries before the ministry of Jesus.

Paula Fontana Qualls

A New Era
LUKE 4:21

ἤρξατο δὲ λέγειν πρὸς αὐτοὺς ὅτι Σήμερον πεπλήρωται ἡ γραφὴ αὕτη ἐν τοῖς ὠσὶν ὑμῶν.

For those who write in English, there are a number of ways that we highlight the importance of a word, phrase, or sentence. We can use UPPERCASE, *italics*, or **boldface** to provide emphasis. Of course, we can also use punctuation marks! Those, like Luke, who wrote in Koine Greek in the first century, did not have these options available to them. Nonetheless, they could still draw attention to words and phrases by means of word choice, word order, and word tense.

In Luke 4:21 the Evangelist employs these strategies to draw our awareness to a significant moment in Jesus's life and ministry. After returning in the power of the Spirit from his wilderness temptations (v. 14), Jesus began teaching in Galilee and came into his hometown synagogue in Nazareth on the Sabbath day (vv. 15–16). After being given the Isaiah scroll, he read from the passage that declared "the Spirit of the Lord is upon me . . . to bring good news . . . to proclaim freedom . . . to set the oppressed free, to proclaim the year of the Lord's favor" (Isa 61:1–2). Jesus then rolled up the scroll, sat down, and said to those present, "Today this scripture is fulfilled in your hearing" (Luke 4:21 NIV). Jesus declares that a new era has begun with him and the work he is doing.

To highlight the importance of this new era, Luke employs three strategies. First, he carefully chooses words in the narrative leading up to Jesus's declaration. The series of main verbs in vv. 16–17 and 20 are introduced with the conjunction καὶ because they are establishing continuity in the scene for the first major development in the narrative that culminates with δέ in verse 21.[1]

Second, Luke's choice of the word σήμερον and the order of its position at the beginning of Jesus's sentence also emphasize the significance of this moment. This word is a favorite of Luke's; almost half of the forty-one occurrences in the NT are in Luke-Acts (11x in Luke; 9x in Acts). He uses "today" almost like a staccato or exclamation point throughout the Gospel to underscore the significance of an event (see 2:11; 5:26; 19:9; 23:43). In 4:21 this word, placed emphatically at the beginning of Jesus's announcement, draws our attention to the new era of salvation—the eschatological "year" of Jubilee—signaled in the ministry of Jesus. Jesus adds his own personal endorsement of this "good news" to the words that have already been declared at the announcement of his birth (1:31–33) and in the words of his mother, Mary (1:46–55).

Luke adds a final flourish of emphasis by employing the perfect tense with the verb πεπλήρωται. The stress of verbal tense in Greek is less on the *when* of an action and more on the *kind* of action. The perfect tense indicates an action that has occurred in the past and which has ongoing implications in the present time. To bring out this force, a paraphrase of Jesus's sentence might read: "Today this Scripture has been fulfilled and will continue to shape my work and words to come . . . ." The perfect tense is used less frequently than some others; when it occurs, we should pay attention. Moulton reminds us that the perfect tense is "the most important, exegetically, of all the Greek Tenses."[2] The only use of

---

1. Martin M. Culy, Mikeal C. Parsons, and Joshua J. Stigall, *Luke: A Handbook on the Greek Text* (Waco, TX: Baylor University Press, 2010), 135. See also S. Runge, *Discourse Grammar of the Greek New Testament: A Practical Introduction for Teaching and Exegesis* (Peabody, MA: Hendrickson, 2010), 23–36.
2. J. H. Moulton, *A Grammar of New Testament Greek*, 4 vols. (Edinburgh: T&T Clark, 1908), 1:140, quoted in Daniel B. Wallace, *Greek Grammar Beyond the Basics* (Grand Rapids: Zondervan, 1996), 573.

πληρόω in the perfect tense in the Gospel of Luke is here in the words of Jesus, in the synagogue of Nazareth, at the beginning of his public ministry. Another related word (πληροφορέω; "to fill completely," "to fulfill") occurs in the first sentence of the Gospel where Luke announces the things that have been fulfilled—and continue to have consequence—among us in the life of Jesus.

In these three ways—word choice, word order, and the use of the perfect tense—Luke draws our attention to the new era of salvation that Jesus inaugurated in that synagogue. Imagine the hush among the attendees when Jesus said this. A similar hush can fall over our hearts when we appreciate how utterly significant the good news of Jesus was and still is.

Dean Pinter

Simon Peter and *Kyrios*-Click

⁵καὶ ἀποκριθεὶς Σίμων εἶπεν, Ἐπιστάτα, δι᾽ ὅλης νυκτὸς κοπιάσαντες οὐδὲν ἐλάβομεν. . . . ⁸Ἔξελθε ἀπ᾽ ἐμοῦ, ὅτι ἀνὴρ ἁμαρτωλός εἰμι, κύριε.

This beautiful and memorable story relates Jesus's calling of Simon Peter to be a disciple. We witness the moment when Peter decided boldly and radically to leave his occupation as a fisherman to become, in Jesus's words, a fisher of people (Luke 5:10).

This rich story intentionally evokes another famous missionary-calling story—that of Isaiah, who, just like Simon Peter, received a revelation from God that opened his eyes to see himself as sinful and broken and unworthy (Isa 6:5; Luke 5:8). In both stories the called one, who responds to God with humility, receives a message of peace and grace and then a commission to go as God's mouthpiece (Isa 6:7–8; Luke 5:10).

Luke's Greek text drives home this aspect of the story in a subtle but powerful way. When we read the broader context of Luke, we see that 5:1–11 is not the first time Peter has encountered Jesus. In fact, Peter has even hosted Jesus in his home and witnessed Jesus heal his mother-in-law (Luke 4:38–39).

Peter understandably has respect for Jesus, recognizing his power and authority. Therefore, Peter calls him ἐπιστάτης ("master"), here in the form of direct address, the vocative ἐπιστάτα (5:5). (This is one of a group of masculine nouns, all descriptors of someone's role or vocation, that follow the first-declension pattern.) Even so, Jesus is clearly no expert fisherman, and so Peter is somewhat reluctant to follow his nonprofessional advice.

But then Jesus performs this shocking and life-changing miracle of the net-breaking catch of fish! This revelation that Jesus is divine immediately makes Simon Peter see himself clearly as sinful and in need of grace. This heart-transforming revelation is expressed in the changed way in which Peter addresses Jesus; his understanding clicks into place. Rather than calling Jesus by the respectful title ἐπιστάτης, he now calls him by the weighty title κύριος (again in the vocative form, κύριε; 5:8). In the Greek Bible κύριος can be a generic title of respect, but it is also the title used for God himself. In light of the miracle that Jesus has done and the change that Peter has experienced, this change from ἐπιστάτα to κύριε is one of the ways in which Luke communicates who Jesus is as the divine master and Peter's changed understanding of this truth.

Jonathan T. Pennington

Growing on the Way with Jesus

LUKE 17:6

εἶπεν δὲ ὁ κύριος, Εἰ ἔχετε πίστιν ὡς κόκκον σινάπεως, ἐλέγετε ἂν τῇ συκαμίνῳ [ταύτῃ], Ἐκριζώθητι καὶ φυτεύθητι ἐν τῇ θαλάσσῃ· καὶ ὑπήκουσεν ἂν ὑμῖν.

After hearing what seems like an impossible demand from Jesus—like forgiving a fellow believer who offends, even seven times in a day (Luke 17:4; cf. Gen 4:24)—we may feel that there is little else we can do besides utter the apostles' own desperate plea: "Increase our faith!"

The disciples' developing faithfulness is an important subplot in the narrative theology of Luke-Acts. Their progress is not, however, a consistent line of maturation that grows in regular increments. Rather, they will continue to stumble and disappoint up until they are changed by the commission of the risen Lord (Luke 24:45–49) and so finally model the loyal duty for which they plead in 17:5. They do follow Jesus on his way to Jerusalem (9:51; 19:41), walking in his footsteps and in the Way (cf. Acts 9:2; 19:9, 23). Faith and obedience, the core of the disciples' request, are at the heart of following the Way (Luke 7:50; 8:12, 25; 17:19). Does the apostles' request for faith indicate a complete deficiency of what is required at this point?

Jesus's response is as surprising as it is commanding. It is also grammatically puzzling because it mixes up the accepted norms for a conditional sentence. Conditional sentences have an "if" part (called the *protasis*, the conditional premise), and a "then" part (called the *apodosis*, the consequence of the argument). In Greek there are different forms for conditional sentences that indicate different relationships between the supposition (the "if" clause) and its consequent (the "then" clause). A first-class condition has εἰ + the indicative mood in the protasis with a wide range of verb forms possible in the apodosis and makes an assertion for the sake of the argument. A second-class condition has εἰ + imperfect or aorist indicative in the protasis and then ἄν + imperfect or aorist in the apodosis. This is a contrary-to-fact assertion that assumes that the premise is not true for the sake of the argument. Jesus's response to his apostles in Luke 17:6 begins with the protasis of a first-class condition (εἰ + ἔχετε [present indicative]), which then switches in form to a two-part second-class condition in the *apodosis* (ἐλέγετε ἄν, ὑπήκουσεν ἄν).

The manuscript tradition (D 𝔐) even attests that later scribes attempted to make it a consistent second-class conditional form by altering the verb to εἴχετε (imperfect) in the *protasis*. This reading would seem to convey a mild rebuke: "If it were the case that you had faith like a mustard seed [but I assume you all do not], then you would be able to say to this mulberry tree . . . and it would obey you [but this won't now happen]." But what is the force of the more authentically attested, mixed-conditional statement in this context?

Jesus's teaching here is remarkable on several accounts. He anticipates coming offenses within the community of disciples but does not allow for the offenders to shirk responsibility. The Lord expects there to be communal disciplining practices that are motivated by generosity and aimed at reconciliation. Jesus balances the inevitability of coming snares and the warning to those by whom they come with the command to the community to extend forgiveness, even in the face of repeated offenses. (Even those committed in the same day!)

In the face of this demand, the apostles recognize their need for more faith. Jesus's answer comes in two parts. First, Jesus utters a mixed-conditional sentence, indicating that even the smallest amount of faith could produce supernatural results: by the word of command a mulberry tree could be uprooted and planted in the sea. (Does this hint at even life and growth possibly coming from an offender ejected into the sea, 17:2?) As a mixed-conditional sentence, the "if" part (in the form of a first-class condition) makes no assessment about the disposition of the apostles' faith, but the "then" part (in the form of a second-class condition) would seem to indicate that the faith is lacking. Is Jesus denying that the apostles have even the smallest amount of faith, not even that of the size of a mustard seed?

Here is where the narrative context gives us a clue. It is not that even the smallest hint of faith or trust is absent. The apostles have after all remained with Jesus, even through various conflicts and antagonisms (5:30, 33; 6:2; cf. 6:22–23). Despite a checkered past (and immediate future) of failures and misunderstandings, what remains to be seen—and what appears to be indicated by the apodosis of Jesus's response—is the need for the *demonstration* of behavior that displays faith. This is, after all, what is appropriate for their place as *slaves* of the Lord (17:7–10) and what is consonant with the disposition of gratitude that flows from receiving the salvation given by Jesus (17:19). As a disciple makes his or her path along the way of the Lord, they must develop habits and behaviors that are the proper follow-through to their confession and their request. Faith requires obedience. The Lord Jesus patiently reminds his followers of this truth with hopeful assurance.

David R. McCabe

The Vindication and Restoration of Zacchaeus

LUKE 19:8

σταθεὶς δὲ Ζακχαῖος εἶπεν πρὸς τὸν κύριον, Ἰδοὺ τὰ ἡμίσειά μου τῶν ὑπαρχόντων, κύριε, τοῖς πτωχοῖς δίδωμι, καὶ εἴ τινός τι ἐσυκοφάντησα ἀποδίδωμι τετραπλοῦν.

Beginning Greek students are taught (rightly, no doubt) to insert a present-tense English verb whenever translating a Greek present-tense verb, at least as a first effort. However, there are several options for understanding the syntax of a present-tense verb in Greek, and Luke 19:8 illustrates at least two of the possibilities. Each syntactical choice leads to a different (theological, narratival, etc.) reading of the Zacchaeus story in Luke 19:1–10, where there are two present tense verbs—δίδωμι and ἀποδίδωμι—that contain such an ambiguity. They may be futuristic presents, which Wallace describes as a present-tense verb used to depict a future event with connotations of immediacy and certainty.[1] However, another option is to see these verbs as customary presents (again using Wallace's category), which have the sense of regularly repeated (and thus customary) action *in the present (as opposed to future) time.*[2]

---

1. Daniel B. Wallace, *Greek Grammar Beyond the Basics* (Grand Rapids: Zondervan, 1996), 535–37.
2. Ibid., 521–22.

Zacchaeus's encounter with Jesus occurs near the end of Luke's famous "travel narrative" that begins at 9:51. The story of this man Zacchaeus, who is either small in stature or small in age (i.e., young), follows a string of carefully designed passages in Luke 18 that encapsulate Jesus's inclusion and preferential treatment of the lowly, including a widow, a tax collector, children, and a blind beggar (though also present is the story of Jesus's conversation with the rich ruler, who serves as a counterpoint to Zacchaeus).

Zacchaeus's own characterization is mixed, even by Lukan standards. We are told that he is wealthy (19:2), and Luke consistently portrays the wealthy negatively in his Gospel. However, Luke almost always depicts tax collectors positively as those who truly see and hear Jesus even though that occupation would marginalize them in the Jewish society of the day. This is affirmed by the crowd's negative response to Jesus's desire to stay with Zacchaeus; they grumble and call Zacchaeus a sinner (vv. 5–7).

In verse 8, Zacchaeus gives a response that is technically addressed to Jesus as Lord but also serves as Zacchaeus's defense against the complaint of the crowd. He states that he "gives" (δίδωμι) half of his possessions to the poor, and if he has defrauded anyone, he "gives back" (ἀποδίδωμι) four times the amount. If these two verbs are futuristic presents, they function as statements of repentance for Zacchaeus; from this point onward he pledges to respond in these ways with his financial resources as evidence of his commitment to Jesus and the kingdom of God.

However, in light of Luke's characterization of Zacchaeus's status as lowly (evidenced through his tax-collecting vocation and the crowd's response in labeling him a sinner) as well as the *lack* of any call to Zacchaeus to repent (cf. the rich ruler in 18:18–30), it is perhaps more likely that these are customary present-tense verbs that indicate an already *existing, ongoing* pattern of behavior in Zacchaeus's life. He truly *sees* (a favorite Lukan theme) and has been embodying the values of the kingdom that Jesus brings.

And Jesus's response is to declare that "today" salvation has come to Zacchaeus's house (v. 9). This salvation, then, is in keeping with Luke's larger narrative: salvation is not "merely" spiritual or vertical (as that has already occurred in Zacchaeus's life) but is horizontal, for Zacchaeus has been welcomed and included in the community of the people of God by Jesus himself. He is not lowly or on the margins but is *vindicated* by Jesus and restored to the circle of the true children of Abraham (v. 9; cf. John the Baptist's challenge in 3:10–17).

Holly Beers

Jesus's Prayer of Thanksgiving

JOHN 11:41

Πάτερ, εὐχαριστῶ σοι ὅτι ἤκουσάς μου.

When Martha warned Jesus, Κύριε, ἤδη ὄζει (v. 39; NRSV: "Already there is a stench"), she meant that there had passed four days of decomposition or putrefaction. If the raising of Lazarus had been an example of genuine resurrection, there would have been no problem about the transformation of such earthly decay into heavenly glory.

On that point Paul declared, "You do not sow the body that is to be. . . . God gives it a body as he has chosen" (1 Cor 15:37–38 NRSV). He continues in verse 44, "It is sown a physical body, it is raised a spiritual body." The NRSV, however, is misleading at this point. The phrase σῶμα ψυχικόν means an *ordinary* body, in accordance with his use of it in 1 Corinthians; similarly, σῶμα πνευματικόν means "of the *Spirit*"; in other words, animated and characterized by the Holy Spirit—again, in accordance with its use in 1 Corinthians. But genuine resurrection could not occur until Jesus Christ had been raised as the firstfruits of the raised community. Jesus restored Lazarus to life presumably in an earthly body to live a prolonged number of years of life under *earthly* conditions before his eventual death. How, then, do we explain the reversal of the effects of decomposition?

The answer appears to lie in the use of the *aorist* in the clause

47

ἤκουσάς μου (John 11:41). This could not have been a "prophetic perfect" of certainty. The aorist in this context carries a reference to past time and a *past event*. Scores of commentators emphasize the *past* act, including A. T. Robinson, R. E. Brown, R. Bultmann, and others. Jesus had *already* prayed to God several days earlier when he was told of Lazarus's death. God had *already* heard him, before the striking public miracle of verse 43. In other words, while Martha understandably assumed that decomposition had taken place, Jesus knew better. Hence the restoration of Lazarus to ordinary life entailed no last-minute reversal of a natural process. Jesus restored to life a body for which he had already prayed to God for the cessation of decomposition. The public miracle of the raising of Lazarus was the climax of a process which had began earlier.

If Christian believers are to take Jesus as their example in prayer, among everything else, prayer should not be a last resort in the face of crisis unless this must be the case of necessity. We should be praying in advance of a future crisis, whether to modify or to forestall it. Prayer requires patience and foresight, as in John 11:41. Further, Jesus lived in constant prayer and communication with his Father. When he engaged in public prayer, he was not entering into prayer from a condition of not praying but was giving overt expression to what was the basis and ground of his life. Similarly, Paul urges us to pray constantly (e.g., Rom 12:12; 1 Thess 5:17).

As a bonus to all this, there need be no puzzlement about the double miracle of restoration to life and the reversal of decomposition. Martha had failed to realize that what she saw as a disastrous delay had already been dealt with by Jesus in his love for the Bethany family of Lazarus and in previous communication with his ever-present Father.

Anthony C. Thiselton

When Heaven Thundered

JOHN 12:27–33

²⁷Νῦν ἡ ψυχή μου τετάρακται. καὶ τί εἴπω; Πάτερ, σῶσόν με ἐκ τῆς ὥρας ταύτης; ἀλλὰ διὰ τοῦτο ἦλθον εἰς τὴν ὥραν ταύτην. ²⁸πάτερ, δόξασόν σου τὸ ὄνομα. ἦλθεν οὖν φωνὴ ἐκ τοῦ οὐρανοῦ, Καὶ ἐδόξασα καὶ πάλιν δοξάσω. ²⁹ὁ οὖν ὄχλος ὁ ἑστὼς καὶ ἀκούσας ἔλεγεν βροντὴν γεγονέναι· ἄλλοι ἔλεγον, Ἄγγελος αὐτῷ λελάληκεν. ³⁰ἀπεκρίθη καὶ εἶπεν Ἰησοῦς, Οὐ δι᾽ ἐμὲ ἡ φωνὴ αὕτη γέγονεν ἀλλὰ δι᾽ ὑμᾶς. ³¹νῦν κρίσις ἐστὶν τοῦ κόσμου τούτου, νῦν ὁ ἄρχων τοῦ κόσμου τούτου ἐκβληθήσεται ἔξω· ³²κἀγὼ ἐὰν ὑψωθῶ ἐκ τῆς γῆς, πάντας ἑλκύσω πρὸς ἐμαυτόν. ³³τοῦτο δὲ ἔλεγεν σημαίνων ποίῳ θανάτῳ ἤμελλεν ἀποθνήσκειν.

The scenes recorded in John 12 bring the curtain down on the public ministry of Jesus. Here we see him speak his last words to the crowd and and then hide himself from view (v. 36). The coming of the Greeks, asking to interview Jesus, marks the arrival of the appointed "hour" (v. 23). The "hour" is nothing less than the appointed time for Jesus's death, resurrection, and exaltation—in short, his glorification. Now, dramatically, the request of the Greeks changes the clock. The shadows of death fell over Jesus, and he was deeply troubled (v. 27). His agonizing prayer closing with the resolve, "Father, glorify your name," was answered with a thundering sound from heaven (v. 28). Some heard what they believed to be thunder; others heard audible speech—that of an angel (v. 29). Both alike were wrong. The thunder of heaven was the voice of God, a direct answer to Jesus's petition: "I have glorified it, and I will glorify it again" (v. 28). What was garbled for the crowd was intended for their benefit, a witness to the significance of that hour, that prayer, and that inquiry from the Greeks.

On the one hand, the sound of thunder is no surprise; thunder signifying God's majestic presence is commonplace in Scripture, as when Israel trembled at Sinai's storm of thunder and lightning (Exod 19:16; cf. Job 37:2–5; Pss 18:11–13; 29:3–4; Rev 4:5; 8:5; 11:19; 16:18). But, on the other hand, we are surprised that this episode—the arrival of the Greeks—should ignite such a startling response. The divine voice (φωνή, "voice" or "sound") was heard on two important occasions in Jesus's ministry: the baptism and the transfiguration. At each of these momentous events the Father's voice, distinct and measured, embraced the Son (Mark 1:11; 9:7). Yet there is no thunder. In contrast, one gets the impression of power, majesty, and glory in the thundering voice of John 12. Surely it is a portent of something vitally important that God should roar his endorsement from heaven's throne.

Heaven thunders assurance for a troubled heart. In v. 27, after the deliberative subjunctive "What shall I say?" (καὶ τί εἴπω;), most versions understand another question, "Father, save me from this hour?" (NIV, NRSV, NASB, ESV, JB, GNB, NA28/UBS5), making the words a thought that Jesus refused to pray. But a positive prayer (KJV, RV, NEB, WH, SBLGNT, reading a full stop after ταύτης, "Father, save me from this hour") fully accords with the Gethsemane prayer, "Take this cup from me" (Mark 14:36), and reflects the troubled soul of Jesus. The word "trouble" (perfect of ταράσσω) signifies revulsion, horror, anxiety, and agitation, a fearful foreboding of the death that loomed on the horizon (John 12:27; cf. 11:33; 13:21). The Father's voice both affirms the Son's courage and points to coming glory. Jesus endured the "hour" so that we need not be troubled (Μὴ ταρασσέσθω ὑμῶν ἡ καρδία, "Do not let your hearts be troubled"; John 14:1).

Heaven thunders the overthrow of the dark empire. With his exaltation, Jesus dethroned the prince of this world. This dramatic development twice comes under a powerful "now" (νῦν, v. 31). "Now" emphasizes the final nature of the events that are impending. The judgment of the world and the destruction of Satan—these might all be reserved for the end times, but the end times have already begun. The decisive step has been taken. In the cross the ruler of this world has been "already judged" (κέκριται, 16:11).

Heaven thunders the power of Jesus's cross to draw all people. The Greeks are harbingers of the harvest to come. The death of Jesus, like seeds that fall into the ground, produces "much fruit" (12:24). By his cross he draws all to himself, no matter how unexpected, calling them out of darkness into light.

Bruce Corley

Recognizing Tense and Mood—and Believing Jesus's Promise

ACTS 1:6–8

⁶Οἱ μὲν οὖν συνελθόντες ἠρώτων αὐτὸν λέγοντες, Κύριε, εἰ ἐν τῷ χρόνῳ τούτῳ ἀποκαθιστάνεις τὴν βασιλείαν τῷ Ἰσραήλ; ⁷εἶπεν δὲ πρὸς αὐτούς, Οὐχ ὑμῶν ἐστιν γνῶναι χρόνους ἢ καιροὺς οὓς ὁ πατὴρ ἔθετο ἐν τῇ ἰδίᾳ ἐξουσίᾳ· ⁸ἀλλὰ λήμψεσθε δύναμιν ἐπελθόντος τοῦ ἁγίου πνεύματος ἐφ᾽ ὑμᾶς, καὶ ἔσεσθέ μου μάρτυρες ἔν τε Ἰερουσαλὴμ καὶ ἐν πάσῃ τῇ Ἰουδαίᾳ καὶ Σαμαρείᾳ καὶ ἕως ἐσχάτου τῆς γῆς.

Jesus's answer to his followers' question in Acts 1:6 is widely recognized as significant for understanding the book of Acts—some scholars consider that it functions as a "table of contents" for the missional narrative which follows in the rest of the book. Their question is entirely understandable in this situation. Given that God has raised Jesus from the dead, what is to follow for God's people, Israel, and for the Eleven, who have been promised that they will rule over Israel (Luke 22:30)?

Jesus gives a most striking answer, in two parts. In the first, he reshapes their assumption that the timing of events is the crucial thing. Rather than wondering whether the restoration of Israel's kingdom will take place "at this time" (ἐν τῷ χρόνῳ τούτῳ), the disciples should leave such questions in God's hands: "It is not for you to know the times and seasons that the Father has set by his own authority" (v. 7).

We shall focus on the second part of Jesus's answer (v. 8), for the choices of verb tense and mood here are significant. This part contrasts with the first and is signaled by the strong adversative ἀλλά ("but"); here is the important part of his response, the part to which they (and we, as Luke's readers) need to pay close attention. Jesus's response here centers on two verbs, λήμψεσθε, "you shall receive," and ἔσεσθε, "you shall be." Both are future indicatives, signaling that the events of which Jesus speaks are yet to take place. By choosing future indicatives, Luke indicates that Jesus is promising that these events *will* take place.

This is striking, for it is all too easy to read this passage through the lens of the Great Commission in Matthew 28, and to treat Acts 1 as though it is saying the same thing as Matthew. In Matthew 28:18–19 the central verb is an aorist imperative, μαθητεύσατε, "make disciples," and participles cluster around it to fill out the picture: they are to "go" (πορευθέντες), and the means of making disciples will be "baptizing" people (βαπτίζοντες) and "teaching" them (διδάσκοντες).[1] Matthew offers a clear *instruction* from Jesus to his followers about how they are to act after his ascension and exaltation.

By contrast, Luke presents a *promise* from Jesus, stated using these future, indicative verbs, and similarly filled out by participles. Rather than exhorting the disciples to "do mission," Jesus here promises two things to them. First, "you will receive power" (λήμψεσθε δύναμιν)—this is the role of the Holy Spirit, for it is when the Spirit comes (aorist participle, ἐπελθόντος) that they will receive power. The temporal signal of the participle's aorist tense form is that the Spirit's coming is first and the receiving of power comes after (or with) the Spirit's coming. The Pentecost

---

1. See the valuable discussion by Craig L. Blomberg, "The Great Commission," in *Devotions on the Greek New Testament: 52 Reflections to Inspire and Instruct*, ed. J. Scott Duvall and Verlyn D. Verbrugge (Grand Rapids: Zondervan, 2012), 24–26.

story vividly describes this happening (Acts 2:1–4). Second, "you will be my witnesses" (ἔσεσθέ μου μάρτυρες), again a future indicative which signals that this *will* happen, for Jesus gives his word. His followers will be empowered by the Spirit and consequently will testify *about* Jesus and testify *with* Jesus (treating the genitive μου as having both an objective- and subjective-genitive nuance).

It would be all too easy to read Matthew's commission on its own, and thus to feel it all depends on us to take the message of Jesus to the nations. That would be a crushing burden. Recognising that in Acts Jesus promises that this *will* take place relieves the pressure, for he does not call us to testify alone but with the Spirit's enabling power.

Steve Walton

Sharing Meals in Public and Private—Watch Those Participles!

ACTS 2:46

καθ᾽ ἡμέραν τε προσκαρτεροῦντες ὁμοθυμαδὸν ἐν τῷ ἱερῷ,
κλῶντές τε κατ᾽ οἶκον ἄρτον, μετελάμβανον τροφῆς ἐν ἀγαλλιάσει
καὶ ἀφελότητι καρδίας

Acts 2:46 is part of a longer section in which Luke sketches key features of the shared life of the earliest believers: apostolic teaching, fellowship, breaking bread, and prayer (2:42–47).

The thing to notice is how the actions of their daily meetings are portrayed using a mix of two participial clauses and a main clause with an indicative verb. Greek participles in narrative add colour and depth to the author's description of a scene and can be related to their main verb (usually an indicative) in a number of ways. Here, the main verb is μετελάμβανον, "they shared," and its object is τροφῆς, "food" (a genitive of the thing shared, as is usual when this verb means "share"). The picture Luke paints is of daily sharing of food among the believers, and he highlights this regularity both by καθ᾽ ἡμέραν, "day by day," and by the use of an imperfect for this main verb, portraying the sharing as iterative (interestingly, this is Luke's only imperfect use of this verb; other uses are aorist).

The participles fill the picture out in striking ways. There are two participles grammatically dependent on this main verb, προσκαρτεροῦντες and κλῶντες. Both are present participles, suggesting that their actions are happening at the same time as the main verb.

The participle προσκαρτεροῦντες ("meeting together") pictures their gatherings in the temple courts (ἐν τῷ ἱερῷ), most probably in the area called Solomon's Portico (5:12), a large covered area inside an outer wall of the temple complex. It would be a natural, open-air venue for the apostles to teach, while also allowing others to "overhear" their teaching and to see the believers' shared life. This participle's dependence on the main verb μετελάμβανον [τροφῆς] "they shared [food]" implies that a feature of their meetings in the temple courts was *eating together*. This echoes Jesus's shared meals, including meals eaten with many who were regarded as "sinners" (e.g., Luke 5:30; 7:34; 15:1–2; 19:7). Jesus's habit scandalized the Pharisees and Jewish leaders (e.g., Luke 7:37–39; 14:12–14). Moreover, believers would not be the only group eating in the temple courts; animal sacrifices were eaten (in part) by the people who offered them (e.g., Lev 7:11–16). By eating together in the temple courts, the believers lived their shared life in public space, open to others' scrutiny. Further, it is highly likely that others were invited and welcomed into these meals, for Jewish people have a strong tradition of hospitality. As others participated in the believers' shared meals, they would encounter the believers' shared life and shared encounter with God through Jesus and by the Spirit. Living the gospel message in public in this way was powerfully attractive: "Every day the Lord was adding to their number those being saved" (Acts 2:47).

The second participle, κλῶντες . . . ἄρτον ("breaking . . . bread"), portrays a central action of the believers' life. Luke records that breaking bread was not a public action, but took place κατ᾽ οἶκον ("in houses"). This was a more private sharing of food than in the temple courts and includes two features: first, further shared meals (since this participle is also dependent on the main verb μετελάμβανον), and, second, the specific remembering of Jesus in the Eucharist or Lord's Supper (the phrase "breaking bread" echoes Jesus's institution of the Eucharist at the last supper; see Luke 22:19; cf. 24:30). Their "breaking bread" would not look like the way many modern churches do this, eating only a token piece of bread and drinking a sip of wine; rather, the remembrance of and giving thanks for the Lord's death would be part of the shared private meals in believers' homes.

Between these two participial clauses, we see both a place for public sharing and generosity in the temple courts and also a place for more intimate sharing and engagement with other believers around the Lord's table in homes. How might your church's life be different if these were both seriously contextualized into today's society and world?

Steve Walton

God's Redemptive Economy of the Gift

ROMANS 5:6

ἔτι γὰρ Χριστὸς ὄντων ἡμῶν ἀσθενῶν ἔτι κατὰ καιρὸν ὑπὲρ ἀσεβῶν ἀπέθανεν.

How often have we heard that we do not deserve God's love but rather only punishment, pain, torment, and retribution for all our sins? While Paul takes sin and its ultimate consequences with utmost seriousness, he does not give us a gospel where our worth or "just deserts" are based on our behaviors or our status as finite and failing beings. Rather, Paul proclaims a gospel where God shows how he values humanity, based on who Christ is and what he has accomplished in his sacrificial death and victorious resurrection.

Indeed, there is a way of being human that is defined by sin (which leads to more sin) that results in death (Rom 5:12–14). Paul uses an economic metaphor of wages and earnings and getting what we deserve to describe what the toil of life is like apart from Christ (Rom 4:2–4). Left simply to ourselves to exchange and commerce within this economy, our lives are degraded and corrupted, so that death can be counted as "just deserts," a wage rightly earned (6:23).

However, Paul uses these economic images precisely in order to contrast them with his gospel message of grace. Paul's gospel is not predicated upon God's act of pitting his compassionate

58

mercy over against his just judgment. Rather, God's grace has shattered this plotline of "just deserts" precisely in order to present an economy centered on the gracious gift of his Son in obedient death and vindicated resurrection: "The free gift is not like the trespass" (5:15)!

Paul presents a divine interruption of the status quo, and he does so using some awkward grammatical turns of phrase. He starkly distinguishes the way things have been from the situation in the current "now" (see νυνὶ δέ in 3:21; cf. 3:26; 5:9, 11; 8:1). In Romans 5:6 we see Paul stress that the gift is given without any regard for the status or earned wage of the receivers. In fact, we see a downward-spiraling regression of identifying markers of the recipients of God's gracious gift:

> "weak" (ἀσθενής, 5:6a)
>> "impious" (ἀσεβής, 5:6b)
>>> "sinners" (ἁμαρτωλός, 5:8)
>>>> "enemies" (ἐχθρός, 5:10).

He begins this sequence in 5:6 with an abrupt grammatical pause (ἔτι), only to repeat it again after a genitive absolute (ὄντων ἡμῶν ἀσθενῶν), which later led to some scribal head-scratching and attempts at improvement (e.g., the initial ἔτι is changed to εἴ γε in Codex Vaticanus [B]). But in the text as it now stands, ἔτι carries the sense of emphasizing the "yet" or "while" that it was the case that humans were weak and impious and sinners—yes, even *then!*—Christ died. Even then, while we were hostile enemies, God showed his love and reconciled us to himself through the death of his precious, righteous Son.

This stands in glaring contrast to the dominant imperial ideology reflected in Roman public transcripts written for dealing with the same groups of people. The weak were to be dominated. The impious were to be subjugated. The sinners were to be chastised. The enemies were to be vanquished. This economic relationship also dominated Rome's disposition toward whole nations in a way that demanded tribute for its "gift" of the *Pax Romana*, which often came at the end of the sword.

Paul's astonishing proclamation of the gospel of Christ is a different thing altogether. Even while all these negative attributes were true of humanity, God's gift comes without regard for status or worth. It obliterates the economy of "just deserts" and establishes peace and reconciliation and hope, so that even the boasting that is denied us (καύχησις, 3:27—4:8) has been redeemed so that we can boast (καυχώμεθα) "in our hope of sharing in the glory of God" (5:2; cf. 8:28–30).

God has demonstrated radical grace in that he has dealt disproportionately and asymmetrically with humans, giving life, salvation, and reconciliation where there was impiety, offense, and hostility. Humanity's worth is now completely redefined in light of God's gracious gift of love. No longer do we wallow in the ineptitude of our weakness. No longer are we crippled by arrogant impiety. No longer are we merely mired in the stains of sin and failure. No longer must we "kick against the goads" and fight against God and his will for the common good. Human beings are not worthless, filthy, nasty, godforsaken degenerates who are worth little more than pond scum. No; rather, our value and worth are granted to us by God's invaluable gift of the Son and the reconciliation available "through his blood." We are now, through the Son, by the Spirit, the very children of God (8:14–17)!

David R. McCabe

Jesus's Death "for Sin"

ROMANS 8:3

τὸ γὰρ ἀδύνατον τοῦ νόμου, ἐν ᾧ ἠσθένει διὰ τῆς σαρκός, ὁ θεὸς
τὸν ἑαυτοῦ υἱὸν πέμψας ἐν ὁμοιώματι σαρκὸς ἁμαρτίας καὶ περὶ
ἁμαρτίας κατέκρινεν τὴν ἁμαρτίαν ἐν τῇ σαρκί

A cademics love them. Students loathe them. To what do I
refer? Footnotes, of course. Footnotes usually have important information. This is especially the case when they appear in
Bibles. A significant example is Romans 8:3. In the main text of
the NIV it reads: "For what the law was powerless to do because
it was weakened by the flesh, God did by sending his own Son in
the likeness of sinful flesh to be a sin offering." In place of "to be
a sin offering," the footnote offers "for sin." Now, the difference
might seem minor, for after all is the "sin offering" not intended
to deal with sin? But herein lies the problem: Does Paul intend an
allusion to the sacrifice known as "the sin offering"? At dispute
here is what the phrase περὶ ἁμαρτίας means. Several issues are
worth thinking about.

First, we can investigate how this phrase is used in the Greek
translation of the Old Testament (LXX). As the argument is usually put, this phrase occurs fifty-four times in the Old Testament,
and at least forty-four of them refer to the sacrifice known as the
sin offering.[1] A good example is Leviticus 5:7 NIV: "Anyone who
cannot afford a lamb is to bring two doves or two young pigeons

---

1. See, for example, N. T. Wright, *The Climax of the Covenant: Christ and the Law in
Pauline Theology* (Minneapolis: Fortress, 1993), 222.

61

to the Lord as a penalty for their sin—one for a sin offering [LXX: περὶ ἁμαρτίας] and the other for a burnt offering." Additionally, of the eight occurrences of the phrase in the New Testament, three of them clearly denote the sin offering (Heb 10:6, 8; 13:11). This certainly seems like overwhelming evidence that Paul must be referring to the sin offering in Romans 8:3. However, what is rarely pointed out is that when this phrase indicates the sin offering, the context is always addressing cultic issues. The phrase itself does not carry the connotation of sin offering; instead, the context gives the phrase this meaning. This raises a second question: Does anything in the context of Romans 8 suggest that Paul is drawing upon a cultic image?

Second, unlike the author of the letter to the Hebrews, Paul does not often use cultic images. Some argue that Romans 3:25 and 5:1–11 have cultic imagery, establishing a pattern so that one might expect to see a cultic image in 8:3. But even in these possible examples, the motif is not absolutely certain. More significantly, there are no clear cultic images in 8:1–4. If Paul intends a reference to the sin offering, it has been very allusive, so allusive that many of his interpreters should be forgiven for not seeing it.

Third, we should take note of the purpose of the sin offering. Despite the implication that the sin offering deals with "sin," its primary purpose was not to address acts of disobedience. Instead, as Leviticus 5 makes clear this offering addresses a state of impurity (e.g., touching a corpse) or mistakes (e.g., taking an oath thoughtlessly). Thus, the two options of "sin offering" and "for sin" would speak of different solutions to different problems.

So what does all this mean? I suggest that the expression περὶ ἁμαρτίας should be understood as a general reference to sin. It parallels other statements about Jesus's death being "for sin(s)" (e.g., Rom 4:25; 1 Cor 15:3; 2 Cor 5:21; Gal 1:4). Such a general reading, in fact, fits comfortably in the context of Romans 7–8. Paul has described a great sinner in Romans 7:7–25, a person ruled by the power of sin, held captive, and dying. To resolve this human dilemma, God does not stand far off. Rather, he enters into the messy world by sending his Son "in the likeness of sinful flesh" (8:3; note the allusion back to 7:14). In this incarnate state, with all its problems, the Son of God addresses the problem of sin, destroys its hold on us, and brings us life and forgiveness. He came "for sin."

Jason Maston

The Process of Sanctification

ROMANS 12:2, 4–5

²καὶ μὴ συσχηματίζεσθε τῷ αἰῶνι τούτῳ, ἀλλὰ μεταμορφοῦσθε τῇ ἀνακαινώσει τοῦ νοός, εἰς τὸ δοκιμάζειν ὑμᾶς τί τὸ θέλημα τοῦ θεοῦ. . . . ⁴καθάπερ γὰρ ἐν ἑνὶ σώματι πολλὰ μέλη ἔχομεν, τὰ δὲ μέλη πάντα οὐ τὴν αὐτὴν ἔχει πρᾶξιν, ⁵οὕτως οἱ πολλοὶ ἓν σῶμά ἐσμεν ἐν Χριστῷ, τὸ δὲ καθ᾽ εἷς ἀλλήλων μέλη.

Although sanctification or growth in holiness may involve one or more decisive events, in the biblical writings it usually constitutes a gradual *process*. Hence Paul uses *present* imperatives. He says, "Stop being conformed to the world," and, "Go on being transformed." J. B. Phillips has the well-known translation or paraphrase, "Don't let the world around you squeeze you into its own mould."

Traditionally we have been taught to believe that σχῆμα compounds (e.g., συσχηματίζεσθε) denote outward or skin-deep appearance, whereas μορφ compounds (e.g., μεταμορφοῦσθε) denote genuine likeness. However, as C. E. B. Cranfield comments, "There are too many examples of [μορφή and σχῆμα] being apparently treated as simply synonymous for it to be justifiable to assume that a distinction is intended unless the context gives support to the assumption."[1] Yet there remains a grain of truth in the traditional comment. F. W. Danker comments that μετασχηματίζω

---

1. C. E. B. Cranfield, *Romans*, 2 vols., ICC (London: T&T Clark, 2004), 2:607.

may denote "to be what one is not," while μεταμορφόω means "to change in a manner visible to others," or "to change inwardly in fundamental character"[2] Furthermore, the *present*, in contrast to the aorist, denotes a *continuous process*. This transformation has as its ultimate cause the Holy Spirit, and as its mediate cause the mental capacities of the mind, including constant reflection and thought (τῇ ἀνακαινώσει τοῦ νοός). Roy Harrisville speaks here of the power of renewal to crowd out the old dynamically.[3] Such transformation and renewal is to have as our goal to rectify our old relationship with the world and to transform and nourish our relationship with Christ and with fellow believers, who are to be respected and welcomed as coequals in the church.

Paul then explains our relationship to other Christians by using the analogy of the body and its "members," a metaphor that was well-known in the Greco-Roman world of Paul's day. However, since in English the word "member" can connote membership in a society or club, commentators such as J. A. T. Robinson have argued that "limbs" would be a far better translation of μέλη: Paul is speaking of an integrally related body with limbs. Without limbs there would scarcely exist a body.[4] As Dale Martin argues, the purpose of this analogy has the reverse function that it has in most Roman authors, including Livy, who uses it to persuade slaves and the oppressed to be obedient to the Senate and slave owners.[5] Paul uses it, by contrast, to cause us to reflect on the status of those whom we might be tempted to regard as socially the lowest or second-class Christians or even outsiders. The analogy thus encourages the deepest solidarity, care, and respect for those who are otherwise regarded as inferior or second-class Christians.

Anthony C. Thiselton

2. BDAG 639, 641.
3. Roy Harrisville, "The Concept of Newness in the New Testament," *JBL* 74.2 (1955): 69–79.
4. J. A. T. Robinson, *The Body: A Study in Pauline Theology* (London: SCM, 1952), 58 and 78–79.
5. Dale B. Martin, *The Corinthian Body* (New Haven: Yale University Press, 1995), 38–63, 94–103; see Livy, *Ab urbe condita* 2.32.7–11, referenced by Martin, 93.

A Dislocated Doxology

ROMANS 16:25–27

²⁵Τῷ δὲ δυναμένῳ ὑμᾶς στηρίξαι κατὰ τὸ εὐαγγέλιόν μου καὶ τὸ κήρυγμα Ἰησοῦ Χριστοῦ, κατὰ ἀποκάλυψιν μυστηρίου χρόνοις αἰωνίοις σεσιγημένου ²⁶φανερωθέντος δὲ νῦν διά τε γραφῶν προφητικῶν κατ᾽ ἐπιταγὴν τοῦ αἰωνίου θεοῦ εἰς ὑπακοὴν πίστεως εἰς πάντα τὰ ἔθνη γνωρισθέντος, ²⁷μόνῳ σοφῷ θεῷ διὰ Ἰησοῦ Χριστοῦ ᾧ ἡ δόξα εἰς τοὺς αἰῶνας ἀμήν.

The Greek text printed directly above is the doxology of Paul's expansive and influential letter to the Romans. In this passage of praise, "the only wise God" is glorified for his ability to establish the Roman Christians in keeping with the long-hidden, now-revealed gospel of Jesus Christ that the apostle Paul proclaims, not least among the gentiles.

Curiously, some ancient Greek manuscripts of Romans lack this doxology. Others include it but place it at the conclusion of chapter 14. Still others place it at the end of chapter 15. Additionally, these verses sometimes occur at both the end of chapters 14 and 15 or after chapters 14 and 16, respectively. To compound matters further, this text appears at the end of a few manuscripts that lack chapters 15–16 altogether. Understandably, such variegated textual phenomena confuse and confound students of the letter!

One possible explanation for this floating doxology is that Romans sometimes circulated without chapters 15 and 16 or simply without chapter 16. It is still far from clear, however, why some manuscripts would lack the doxology altogether. Some scholars have wondered if the varied placement of the doxology, the absence of the doxology, and the arguably non-Pauline expressions within the doxology suggest that it was added by a later scribe.

Whatever the case, editors and translators have typically chosen to place the doxology at the conclusion of chapter 16. Given the contents of Romans, it seems wholly appropriate that the letter would end by lauding the Lord who is capable of undergirding people in the gospel regardless of their circumstances, and that this eternal, wise God would be glorified for the revelation of Jesus Christ, particularly to the nations.

What is true of Romans in particular is no less true of the Christian life in general—during hard times, a doxology can sometimes seem out of place. Paul helps us by pointing to three benefits of justification in Romans 5:1–5; we have true and lasting peace, we have perpetual access to unmerited grace, and we have a spiritual understanding of affliction—in which we are instructed to rejoice (v. 3). This theme is echoed later when the believer faces "trouble, hardship, persecution, famine, nakedness, danger, [and] sword" (8:35). Even in the face of suffering that reduces us to "wordless groans" (8:26), however, of this we can be sure: God is good and is at work for the *good* (cf. 8:28). Through it we are becoming more and more like Christ. Indeed, as an earlier doxology in Paul's letter to the Romans exclaims, "For from him and through him and for him are all things. To him be the glory forever! Amen" (11:36 NIV). Whatever comes our way, may we never be found wanting for an appropriate doxology.

Todd D. Still

Hidden from Plain Sight

I CORINTHIANS 1:18–25

Understanding how a passage is put together is critical to a correct interpretation of the text. Far too often the connectors between units of thought are neglected or ignored, leaving the door open for reading one's own predetermined structure into the passage as though it was there originally. Seldom, if ever, is this correct. The apostle Paul especially loved causal connectors, as is reflected in primary ideas with γάρ ("for"; 379x in Paul, with eighty-three of ninety-five uses causal in 1 Cor) and in secondary ideas with ὅτι ("because"; thirty-nine uses are causal of 255 total uses in Paul's writings, with ten in 1 Cor). These connectors function as conjunctions, while εἰς functions often in the same role as a preposition ("for"; eighty-seven times causal of 408 Pauline uses, with nine of sixteen as causal uses in 1 Cor). Let's see how this works in Paul's definitive passage on the cross at 1 Corinthians 1:18–25:

¹⁸   γάρ

                                                  τοῖς μὲν ἀπολλυμένοις

Ὁ λόγος ... μωρία ἐστίν,

        ὁ τοῦ σταυροῦ

    δὲ

                                        τοῖς σῳζομένοις ἡμῖν

(Ὁ λόγος) δύναμις θεοῦ ἐστιν.

¹⁹   γάρ

γέγραπται

        Ἀπολῶ τὴν σοφίαν τῶν σοφῶν,

        καὶ

τὴν σύνεσιν τῶν συνετῶν ἀθετήσω.

20 **ποῦ σοφός;**

ποῦ γραμματεύς;

ποῦ συζητητὴς τοῦ αἰῶνος τούτου;

οὐχὶ ἐμώρανεν ὁ θεὸς τὴν σοφίαν τοῦ κόσμου;

21 γὰρ

ἐν τῇ σοφίᾳ τοῦ θεοῦ

ἐπειδὴ . . . οὐκ ἔγνω ὁ κόσμος διὰ τῆς σοφίας τὸν θεόν,

εὐδόκησεν ὁ θεὸς

διὰ τῆς μωρίας τοῦ κηρύγματος

σῶσαι τοὺς πιστεύοντας.

22 ἐπειδὴ καὶ Ἰουδαῖοι σημεῖα αἰτοῦσιν

καὶ Ἕλληνες σοφίαν ζητοῦσιν,

23 δὲ

ἡμεῖς κηρύσσομεν Χριστὸν ἐσταυρωμένον,

Ἰουδαίοις μὲν σκάνδαλον

δὲ

ἔθνεσιν μωρίαν,

24 δὲ

αὐτοῖς τοῖς κλητοῖς,

Ἰουδαίοις τε καὶ Ἕλλησιν,

Χριστὸν

θεοῦ δύναμιν

καὶ

θεοῦ σοφίαν·

25 ὅτι τὸ μωρὸν τοῦ θεοῦ σοφώτερον τῶν ἀνθρώπων

ἐστίν,

καὶ

τὸ ἀσθενὲς τοῦ θεοῦ ἰσχυρότερον τῶν ἀνθρώπων.

A close examination of 1:18–25 reveals the critical role that connectors played in Paul's thinking about the cross and its connection to wisdom. How does he put his thoughts together in 1:18–25? The diagram visually reveals the pattern of Paul's thought.

The initial γάρ in v. 18 sets up the pericope of vv. 18–25 as a justification of what Paul claimed in vv. 10–17, and especially in v. 17. Thus, the meaning of vv. 18–25 grows directly out of vv. 10–17. As a side note, γάρ in v. 26 connects up vv. 26–31 to vv. 18–25, as application to the Corinthians themselves. He appeals to their background as validation of the claims made about the cross and wisdom in vv. 18–25. One should never ignore this process of linking ideas together in the writings of Paul.

The single, elliptical compound sentence in v. 18 sets forth the core point of vv. 18–25 beginning with τοῖς μὲν ἀπολλυμένοις, who consider the cross as μωρία. On the opposite side stand τοῖς δὲ σῳζομένοις ἡμῖν, who view the cross as δύναμις θεοῦ.

The λόγος is the preaching of Paul that receives mixed responses. Why? Paul answers that with an appeal to Isaiah 29:14. He quotes either from an unknown version of the Septuagint or else he is interpreting the LXX text with some modifications, most notably changing the verb κρύψω, "I will hide," to ἀθετήσω, "I will nullify." The corresponding Hebrew term in Isaiah 29:14 clearly means "to hide." But Paul sees in hiding the meaning of nullifying. Yet the central point of Isaiah 29:14 and its parallel strophe is that God's actions will confound any and all human understanding of them, even the deeper understanding labeled σοφία in the LXX.

Paul then elaborates in vv. 20–25 on how this Old Testament claim justifies his distinction between the two responses to the gospel. The reasoning begins with three, pointed rhetorical questions, in which Paul dares anyone to disagree with him. The fourth rhetorical question in v. 20 is the type of Greek question that expected his audience to agree with his point. Then γάρ introduces an extended justification in vv. 21–25 of the main point behind the rhetorical questions in v. 20. Two core declarations are made in the single sentence of vv. 21–25. These elaborate on the ignorance of human thinking if people use it as the way to God, with the assertion that God chose to save believers through τῆς μωρίας τοῦ κηρύγματος. This gospel message centers on Christ as both ἐσταυρωμένον and θεοῦ δύναμιν καὶ θεοῦ σοφίαν. Paul concludes his commentary on Isaiah 29:14 with the twofold declaration of the superiority of God's wisdom and "weakness" over any human ability. The introductory ὅτι in v. 25 sets this up in a secondary role in order to preserve the primary emphasis on the superiority of Christ as God's wisdom and "weakness" evidenced on the cross.

If a believer can't get excited about God's wisdom hidden from nonbelieving eyes but made crystal clear to believing eyes, then something is seriously wrong with their eyes. We never "know" our way to God. But in faith, we surrender and are granted God's wisdom to see what is really at work. And it's marvelously wonderful!

Lorin L. Cranford

God: Source of All Comfort

2 CORINTHIANS 1:3–4

³Εὐλογητὸς ὁ θεὸς καὶ πατὴρ τοῦ κυρίου ἡμῶν Ἰησοῦ Χριστοῦ, ὁ πατὴρ τῶν οἰκτιρμῶν καὶ θεὸς πάσης παρακλήσεως, ⁴ὁ παρακαλῶν ἡμᾶς ἐπὶ πάσῃ τῇ θλίψει ἡμῶν, εἰς τὸ δύνασθαι ἡμᾶς παρακαλεῖν τοὺς ἐν πάσῃ θλίψει διὰ τῆς παρακλήσεως ἧς παρακαλούμεθα αὐτοὶ ὑπὸ τοῦ θεοῦ.

The word εὐλογητός (v. 3) is the adjective cognate of the verb εὐλογέω and is used here to introduce a praise of God (while εὐχαριστέω in v. 11 is used to express gratitude toward God for his work). Its Hebrew equivalent is *baruk*, Aramaic *berik*, "blessed." It introduces what possibly may be best called a doxology. Paul says with much delight that God gave him special strength in the midst of trials that threatened to overwhelm him. In v. 3, the apostle addresses God twice each as "God" and "Father," although the order is reversed in v. 3b. God is both the "God" and the "Father" of "our Lord Jesus Christ." Yet this God is also the God of πάσης παρακλήσεως, comfort of every kind. It conveys the idea of strengthening, of helping, of making strong. Paul undoubtedly has in mind his devastating affliction in Asia (1:8–10) and his debilitating depression in Troas and Macedonia (2:12–13; 7:5–6).

From the beginning of his Christian life, Paul understood his calling to suffer for the name of Christ (Acts 9:15–16). Suffering for Christ was ever his destiny as the apostle to the gentiles (1 Thess

2:2; cf. Col 1:24; Eph 3:13). Paul calling God "Father of mercies" and "the God of all encouragement" is therefore significant, and it is noteworthy that the former perhaps recalls Exodus 34:6.

Παράκλησις is the key word controlling the discussion in vv. 3–7. Its root is found ten times in these five verses and is also found throughout the epistle. The different renderings are "comfort" (RSV, NIV), "encouragement" (NJB), "consolation" (NEB), and "help" (TEV/GNB). Here the apostle highlights his own experience of the character of God as compassionate and comforting.

In v. 4 Paul illuminates how God *comforts* us in all our afflictions, and as a result we can encourage those who are in any trial by the same encouragement that we ourselves received from God. In 2 Corinthians Paul repeatedly emphasizes comfort, a *consolatory strengthening* in the face of adversity that affords spiritual refreshment, and is not just mere words. It is mediated by fellow believers, but its ultimate source is God (7:6–7, 13). The timeless comforter, *who always comforts*, is depicted here in v. 4. The purpose of God is to enable the one who receives comfort in suffering to in turn comfort others. The reality of God's comfort in Paul's affliction and distress enabled him to redirect the same to those who were facing a difficult situation. His experience not only benefited him, pulling him ever closer to divine care and comfort, but the overflow benefited his fellow believers as well. Paul is not communicating that he himself is the source of comfort; rather, the Christian's experience of God's help, consolation, and encouragement in the midst of life's afflictions constantly qualifies and empowers them to communicate the divine comfort to others who face troubles of all kinds. Interestingly, Epictetus and Seneca referred to this principle also; namely, that one's own experience of suffering can aid those who are in similar situations. Paul applied to his converts the same encouragement he received from God. Paul here acts as a mediator, passing on the comfort to suffering Corinthians. The present tense of παρακαλούμεθα in

v. 4 highlights the constancy and even the predictability of God's comfort: παράκλησις follows θλῖψις as surely as a sunrise follows a sunset. The theme continues to echo throughout 2 Corinthians 1–7, especially in chapter four. In this chapter with eternity clearly in focus, Paul elaborates on the immortal treasure contained in our fragile, earthen vessels.

Susan Mathew

ἡμεῖς δὲ πάντες ἀνακεκαλυμμένῳ προσώπῳ τὴν δόξαν κυρίου κατοπτριζόμενοι τὴν αὐτὴν εἰκόνα μεταμορφούμεθα ἀπὸ δόξης εἰς δόξαν καθάπερ ἀπὸ κυρίου πνεύματος.

    δὲ
        ἀνακεκαλυμμένῳ προσώπῳ
        τὴν δόξαν κυρίου κατοπτριζόμενοι
ἡμεῖς ... πάντες ... τὴν αὐτὴν εἰκόνα μεταμορφούμεθα
        ἀπὸ δόξης
        εἰς δόξαν
        καθάπερ ἀπὸ κυρίου πνεύματος.

Authentic interpretation of the biblical text depends on correctly understanding the relationship between primary and secondary ideas. With Greek syntax being so dramatically different from English, understanding the Greek properly becomes all the more important.

In the concluding sentence of 2 Corinthians 3:12–18, the primary idea is illustrated in the above diagram (v. 18). In the core declaration ἡμεῖς δὲ πάντες ... τὴν αὐτὴν εἰκόνα μεταμορφούμεθα, Paul asserts that we all are being "metamorphosed" into the same image. Contextually, ἡμεῖς δὲ πάντες, "we all," includes those who have turned to the Lord, ἐὰν ἐπιστρέψῃ πρὸς κύριον (v. 16a).

The present tense, first-plural passive verb μεταμορφούμεθα specifies a profound transformation, taking place as an ongoing process over the course of the life of the believer, not a onetime experience. This transformation is a lifetime development that is being done to us (passive-voice verb); we don't achieve it ourselves. The term μεταμορφόω is used of the transfiguration of Jesus in Matthew 17:2 and Mark 9:2 and thus to a onetime event. But in the other two New Testament uses in Romans 12:2 and 2 Corinthians 3:18, it refers to the believer's life being transformed as ongoing experience. The sudden transformation of Jesus reflects the full intensity of the divine presence enveloping Jesus for that moment; believers for their part experience this over a lifetime of repeated experience prior to heaven.

Crucial to this description of our transformation is the term δόξα, used three times in 2 Corinthians 3:18. The vast majority of the New Testament uses of δόξα (149 of 166) refers to the glory of God. The transformation takes place in connection to the level of divine δόξα at work in our lives. Paul "fleshes out" this transformation with five modifying phrases.

First is ἀνακεκαλυμμένῳ προσώπῳ, "with an unveiled face." The reference connects this statement back to vv. 12–17. This is a continuing commentary on how Moses used a veil after encountering the Lord on Mt. Sinai to receive the Torah. Moses covered his face after speaking to the people while his face glowed from having spoken with the Lord on Sinai. The glow faded, and, according to Paul, Moses sought to hide this fading glow from the people so they would not begin to doubt that he had been with the Lord. The veil came to symbolize absence from the Lord. The apostle contends that the hardness of heart of the Israelite people is represented by Moses's veil even into Paul's day whenever the Torah is read in the synagogues (vv. 14–15). The only way for this veil to be removed is by turning to Christ (v. 16). When believers focus on Christ, they experience transformation by having doubt removed from their lives.

Second is τὴν δόξαν κυρίου κατοπτριζόμενοι, "seeing the divine presence of the Lord as reflected in a mirror." This divine presence comes through Christ, who functions as a mirror in reflecting it to the believer. Thus, transformation of life comes in proportion to our gazing into the mirror, who is Christ. The more we focus on him, the greater the transformation of our life.

While these first two modifiers in front of the verb define the means of this transformation, the subsequent three modifiers stress its impact.

The third and fourth are a pair of interconnected prepositional modifiers: ἀπὸ δόξης εἰς δόξαν, "from glory into glory." Contextually from vv. 7–11, the meaning is from the limited glory with Moses to the full glory with Christ. The premise is that the divine presence increases its transforming power the more we focus on Christ. This is essential since ὁ δὲ κύριος τὸ πνεῦμά ἐστιν· οὗ δὲ τὸ πνεῦμα κυρίου, ἐλευθερία, "now the Lord is the Spirit, and where the Spirit of the Lord, there is freedom" (v. 17). Freedom in this case means that the limitations of Torah are removed so that the divine presence can freely operate in transforming us. The Torah puts the responsibility of transformation on us, but the Spirit liberates us from this by taking on the responsibility for transformation himself.

The fifth modifier shows how this works in the comparative phrase καθάπερ ἀπὸ κυρίου πνεύματος, "just as from the Lord, who is the Spirit." The source of this transformation is the Lord, who is the divine Spirit at work in our lives. It's not self-effort but a divine presence that transforms us.

Praise God who changes us and enables us to increasingly experience his presence as we focus our attention increasingly on Christ. This frees up the Holy Spirit to produce this transformation of our lives as an ongoing process all through our journey on earth.

Lorin L. Cranford

Enabling and
Empowering Grace
2 CORINTHIANS 12:9

καὶ εἴρηκέν μοι, Ἀρκεῖ σοι ἡ χάρις μου· ἡ γὰρ δύναμις ἐν ἀσθενείᾳ
τελεῖται. ἥδιστα οὖν μᾶλλον καυχήσομαι ἐν ταῖς ἀσθενείαις μου,
ἵνα ἐπισκηνώσῃ ἐπ᾽ ἐμὲ ἡ δύναμις τοῦ Χριστοῦ.

How do we understand God's power? Often we may expect
God's power to manifest itself in a spectacular way. However, Paul talks about how God's power is manifested in Paul's
own weakness. He requested the removal of Satan's thorn, but it
remained even though he repeatedly (three times) implored God
to intervene (v. 8). However, the answer for the prayer is presented
in a way he never expected—the risen Christ's grace and power
to cope with an otherwise unknown weakness that afflicted him.
(Paul calls it a σκόλοψ, "thorn"; v. 7). Verse 9 is the climax of
12:7–9 and perhaps even of the whole letter. Paul's request was
in reported speech, also known as indirect discourse (v. 8), while
Christ's response is given in direct discourse (v. 9). The use of the
perfect tense in the phrase καὶ εἴρηκέν in v. 9 is in contrast with
the aorist tense in the phrase τὸν κύριον παρεκάλεσα in v. 8.

While Paul says that what he had heard in paradise is both
inexpressible and impermissible to share (v. 4), Christ's reply to
his prayer was both expressible and permissible to share (v. 9).
Verse 9 has two parts: Christ's word and Paul's response. In the
Lord's reply to Paul in v. 9a, he begins with a promise, and then

gives a statement that explains or supports the promise, as indicated by the "explanatory" γάρ.

The ironic contrast is between Christ's power and Paul's weakness. The terms χάρις and δύναμις are effectively synonymous in this context. Both terms pertain to divine empowerment for Paul to accomplish God's will. The present tense of the verbs τελεῖται and ἀρκεῖ is significant, as the empowerment is a continuing process and not a onetime application. As Paul's weakness persists, Christ's power is simultaneously fully present in him. The word ἀσθενείαις does not refer to a generic human weakness but the weakness Paul felt due to the presence of the unnamed σκόλοψ.

The preposition ἐν modifying ταῖς ἀσθενείαις shows that it is in the sphere of weakness that the power is made perfect. The divine enabling will be triggered by the acknowledgment of weakness. Weakness is the sphere of experience in which the power is revealed and active. He states that when he is weak, he experiences power and this helps him to be strong (v. 10b). The greater the acknowledged weakness, the more evident is Christ's power.

Therefore, Paul cheerfully boasts of his weaknesses, in order that the power of Christ may rest upon him. The use of the singular in v. 9b is noteworthy, as he may be alluding to a particular infirmity or disease that was present and unabated in his fleshly body. Paul desires instead to boast of his infirmities rather than complain about them. He's the strongest spiritually when he is the weakest physically. He finds joy in boasting of the weaknesses in his life rather than praying for their removal and boasting of his revelations or his strength. This process is exactly the opposite of what we might find in a worldly person.

So, boasting in weakness is a prerequisite for experiencing Christ's power. The result clause introduced by ἵνα can be rendered "so that the power of Christ may come and *rest upon me*." The verb translated "rest upon," ἐπισκηνώσῃ (from ἐπισκηνόω) is found only here in biblical Greek. Outside Scripture it can mean "raise a tent over," "be quartered in," "take up a residence in a tent or dwelling" (cf. BDAG). Some find an allusion to the Jewish understanding of the Shekinah glory of God's presence. In the Septuagint, the word σκηνή represents both the tent of meeting and the overshadowing of the divine glory. And in John 1:14 the verb σκηνόω is used to describe the incarnation of Christ. There is, therefore, divine enablement, empowering, and protection in Paul as the power of Christ dwells in him. The use of ἡ δύναμις is possibly emphatic: *the* power of Christ may rest upon me. Because of the thorn and its continuous buffeting, Paul all the more experiences the indwelling of the power of Christ and exuberantly boasts in his weaknesses.

Susan Mathew

The Long and the Short of It

εὐαγγελίζηται. . . . εὐαγγελίζεται

Elijah didn't find God in a cliff-shattering wind, a massive earthquake, or a consuming fire. While all three were obviously powerful and potentially devastating forces, God chose instead to speak through a still, small whisper (1 Kgs 19:11–13). Likewise, in Greek sometimes the biggest differences can be seen in a still, small letter. Take, for example, the situation Paul faced immediately following the first missionary journey that saw many gentiles converted to the faith (Acts 13–14). Circumcision-minded Jews from Jerusalem subsequently traveled to missionary headquarters in Antioch, banged hard on the door, and demanded that these new gentile converts undergo the knife of Mosaic ritualism. This threat called for an immediate response from Paul, notably his white-hot emergency letter to the Galatians before taking part in the Jerusalem Council that is recorded in Acts 15. One of my seminary professors, James W. MacGorman, captured the tone of Galatians by comparing it to Romans, a thematically similar letter written most likely a decade later but in a much calmer atmosphere: "If Romans is polished stone, then Galatians is molten lava!"

Let's get to the lava. As one begins reading this letter, there is no warm opening thanksgiving announced for his readers as is his normal style in later letters. He is *amazed* at their quick desertion (1:6), calls them "foolish" (3:1), is *perplexed* (4:20), and even reasons that if circumcision is a necessity for salvation, how much more would *mutilation* or *castration* be (5:12)! Another tell-tale sign that Paul's words are thoroughly soaked in agitation is that the Greek text is marked by suspended grammatical constructions; this is technically known as *anacoluthon*, meaning "it doesn't follow." One can imagine Paul pacing back and forth as he tried to find the words to address this sudden perversion of the gospel he just preached. The situation required a boiling response. Even the careful reader might have trouble seeing the seriousness of the situation in an English translation like that found in the HCSB of Galatians 1:8–9, because this English translation includes *if* in both verses.

> ⁸But even *if* we or an angel from heaven *should preach* (εὐαγγελίζηται) to you a gospel other than what we have preached to you, *a curse be on him* (ἀνάθεμα ἔστω)!
> ⁹As we have said before, I now say again: *If* anyone *preaches* (εὐαγγελίζεται) to you a gospel contrary to what you received, *a curse be on him* (ἀνάθεμα ἔστω)!

The first occurrence of the verb in v. 8, εὐαγγελίζηται, is in the subjunctive mood as indicated by an eta in the verbal ending (long e in English). The sense of what Paul is saying here is that even if one of the members of his missionary team or an angel from heaven should preach something contrary to the original gospel already preached, then that person would invite God's curse. When Paul used ἀνάθεμα, he tapped into the Old Testament idea of *kherem*, meaning that someone or something had been devoted to God for destruction. So, how likely is that Paul would ever have preached another gospel? Not very, but if it did, he saw himself subject to God's judgment.

The second occurrence of the verb in v. 9, εὐαγγελίζεται is different, since it is in the indicative mood as indicated by an epsilon in the verbal ending (short e in English). This is the mood of reality in the Greek New Testament. Someone actually did it! The difference in the two is much more than the almost imperceptible difference in the vocalization of the eta or the epsilon. The Judaizers had placed themselves in the crosshairs of God's ἀνάθεμα because they changed the gospel message of "salvation = faith in Christ + nothing" into "salvation = faith in Christ + circumcision." Paul said earlier that this is not another gospel of the same kind (ἄλλος); it is a gospel of a different kind (ἕτερος) (vv. 6–7).

Unfortunately, this is an error people fall into even today. A *Galatian violation* is committed when we take various kinds of legitimate religious experience and try to make them into necessary requirements for salvation, whether it be baptism, the exercise of some spiritual gift, or in some cases holding to a particular biblical doctrine. The message is still as simple today as it was at the close of the first missionary campaign: call upon the name of the Lord, and you will be saved!

Paul N. Jackson

The Gospel Is a Revelation
GALATIANS 1:16

ἀποκαλύψαι τὸν υἱὸν αὐτοῦ ἐν ἐμοὶ ἵνα εὐαγγελίζωμαι αὐτὸν ἐν τοῖς ἔθνεσιν, εὐθέως οὐ προσανεθέμην σαρκὶ καὶ αἵματι

Paul was upset with his converts in Galatia because they didn't see the gospel of Jesus Christ revealed in him. If they had, they wouldn't have turned to the law of Moses for direction—something for which Paul was once zealous but which no longer defined his life. That's why Paul tells his "life story" in miniature, describing his life before and after the Christophany (Gal 1:11–2:21). What happened to Paul that day changed not only him—the apocalypse of God's Son changed the whole world. As he wrote elsewhere, "if anyone is in Christ, the new creation has come. The old is gone, the new is here!" (2 Cor 5:17). Indeed, the apocalypse of Jesus Christ was an "end-of-the-world event" that redefined Paul, the law, Israel, and even the Galatians.

Take Paul, for example. He used to be zealous for Jewish traditions built on the law—so zealous he once persecuted the church in order to "destroy it" (Gal 1:13–14). But after the Christophany, Paul was set apart like a prophet of God to preach the gospel to the nations, those "outside" Jewish traditions. Paul was a living memorial, the incarnation of the gospel, and an "apocalypse" of Jesus Christ to the gentiles. That's why Paul described his calling as the work of God. Jesus did more than just appear to him. God was pleased "to reveal his Son *in me*" (ἀποκαλύψαι τὸν υἱὸν αὐτοῦ ἐν ἐμοί, v. 16)—the preposition ἐν used here to denote sphere. To be sure, some translate the prepositional phrase ἐν ἐμοί as an indirect object, "to me" (e.g., NRSV, CEB), and indeed, in other places Paul wrote about the Christophany as Christ "appearing to him," for example, in 1 Corinthians 15:8: "And last of all he appeared to me also [ὤφθη κἀμοί]." But in Galatians 1:16, Paul didn't describe the Christophany as Christ merely "appearing to him." Instead, he used the provocative (and to some, rather enigmatic) word ἀποκαλύψαι along with the prepositional phrase ἐν ἐμοί to describe something that happened *to him* ("I saw the resurrected Messiah—it's the end of the world!") and also *in him* ("everything changed the day I met Christ—my identity, my reputation, my former way of life, my view of the law, my view of the world, my purpose for life—old things passed away and everything became new"). The Galatians should have already known that. Yet in case they forgot, he reminded them about the radical, apocalyptic, dramatic change in his life the day he met the king of Israel and of the whole world (1:11–2:21).

It's no wonder, then, that Paul's talk of being "crucified with Christ" (2:20) and bearing on his body "the marks [τὰ στίγματα] of Jesus" (6:17) appears only in Galatians. The apostle to the gentiles believed he was a revelation/apocalypse of the cross of Jesus Christ, the essence of the gospel: "May I never boast except in the cross of our Lord Jesus Christ, through which the world has been crucified to me, *and I to the world*" (6:14 NIV). The gospel was more than a message to proclaim; it was a way of life. Indeed, the cross of Jesus tattooed Paul's body—what he referred to as "the weakness of my flesh" (ἀσθένειαν τῆς σαρκός, 4:13)—something the Galatians should have been repulsed by, but "instead, you welcomed me as if I were an angel of God, as *if I were Christ Jesus himself*" (4:14 NIV). Fittingly, then, Paul used apocalyptic language to describe the cross as God's end-of-the-world revelation of Christ in him that anyone who had "eyes to see" could see—especially his own converts: "You foolish Galatians! Who has bewitched you? *Before your very eyes Jesus Christ was clearly portrayed as crucified*" (3:1 NIV). All they had to do was look at him.

Rodney Reeves

Saved through Faithfulness as God's Gift

EPHESIANS 2:8–9

⁸ᵃτῇ γὰρ χάριτί ἐστε σεσῳσμένοι διὰ πίστεως· ᵇκαὶ τοῦτο οὐκ ἐξ ὑμῶν, ᶜθεοῦ τὸ δῶρον· ⁹ᵃοὐκ ἐξ ἔργων, ᵇἵνα μή τις καυχήσηται.

The conjunctions, modifiers, word order, and word choice in Ephesians 2:8–9 communicate important points about the origins, agency, and purpose of God's salvation. Such a salvation is stressed by using a periphrastic participle construction with a perfect-tense participle in 2:8a; the construction stresses the "having been saved-ness" as a verbal attribute of the subjects. Thus, a close look at 2:8–9 will inform what Paul means in emphasizing believers' "having been saved-ness."

First, the use or absence of conjunctions helps one track the argument's progression. The γάρ in 2:8a is, uncharacteristically, the first one in Ephesians and signals support for 2:4–7, which describes God's loving, merciful, and salvific response to the deadly human condition of oppressive sin in 2:1–3. So, 2:8 provides support by delineating what God has provided for salvation in contrast to what humans have provided. The καί in 2:8b marks continuity with 2:8a; it continues the point. However, the next two clauses in 2:8c and 2:9a lack conjunctions (this is called *asyndeton*). This terse manner of expression indicates here that

Paul is further explicating the specific point of 2:8b, namely, that salvation is God's gift and does not have human origin. Following this, Paul then signals a negative purpose statement with ἵνα μή that denies any basis of human boasting (v. 9b); God's provision of salvation was done with the intent that no human would have any bragging rights over any other as far as bringing or gaining salvation on their own merits.

Second, consider the modifiers and their word order. In 2:8a a dative of means (τῇ χάριτί, "by means of grace/favor") is placed before the main verb ἐστε σεσῳσμένοι for emphasis. As implied in the context, this grace or favor originates with God. Importantly, this verb is further modified by "through faith(fulness)" (διὰ πίστεως). The use of the preposition διά with the genitive often indicates intermediate agency or means—that is, a secondary level of means or agency. Here, this refers to the human response to God's grace (possibly including Christ's exemplary faithfulness). Then, in 2:8b τοῦτο is neuter and singular and so does not refer either to "grace" or "faith" individually (both are feminine in gender) but rather to the whole complex of salvation that involves both the divine initiation of grace and the human response of faith(fulness). Then, in 2:8c Paul continues by clarifying that the origin of salvation is not "from you" but is "*God's* gift." Paul stresses "God's" by placing the genitive θεοῦ in front of its head noun τὸ δῶρον ("gift").

Third, this word "gift" (δῶρον) is a significant biblical word. In the Septuagint it *always* refers to sacrificial gifts offered to God *by humans* (see especially Leviticus), but here at 2:8 Paul uses it for *God's* gracious offer of Christ as the sacrificial gift (see 1:7; 2:13, 16; 5:2, 25). To explicate this point further, Paul in 2:9 explains that human "works (of the law)" play no part in salvation, "in order that [ἵνα] not anyone would boast." The word "works" here is Paul's shorthand for "works *of the law*"; in Romans 2:17, 23 (cf. Gal 6:13) Paul discounts any basis for someone boasting in the law. Thus, in Ephesians 2:8–9 Paul effectively denies that salvation comes from human agency ("from you" and "from works [of the law]") but rather through God's divine accomplishment in Christ Jesus. This truth becomes crystal clear in 2:10, as we shall see in the next devotion.

Fredrick J. Long

God's Masterful Construction Founded in Christ Jesus upon Good Deeds

^{10a}αὐτοῦ γάρ ἐσμεν ποίημα, ^bκτισθέντες ἐν Χριστῷ Ἰησοῦ ἐπὶ ἔργοις ἀγαθοῖς ^cοἷς προητοίμασεν ὁ θεός, ^dἵνα ἐν αὐτοῖς περιπατήσωμεν.

This devotion builds on the previous one, which dealt with Ephesians 2:8–9. In this verse we will pay attention to conjunctions, verbal voice, and key words. The γάρ connecting v. 10 to vv. 8–9 indicates support for Paul's previous point that the origin of salvation is not "from you" but "is *God's* gift, in order that not anyone would boast." Verse 10 is itself a complex sentence with the circumstantial participle κτισθέντες, which builds to its purpose statement, with ἵνα delineating God's ethical goal that saved humans "walk" in good deeds. Paul effectively shows how God reverses the human problem of "walking" in sin (2:1–3) by calling humans to "walk" in good works, following the example of Christ Jesus, the Son of God, the perfect man, and the Messiah. Paul's use of the passive voice within 2:8–10 demonstrates how human transformation occurs through divine origin and agency. Passive voice verbs in 2:8a ("having been saved") and

2:10b ("having been created/founded") refer only to Christians. In 2:8a the perfect, passive, periphrastic construction "you have been saved" (ἐστε σεσῳσμένοι) emphasizes the continuing results of salvation. Earlier in 2:5, Paul had startlingly inserted "having been saved by grace" (χάριτί ἐστε σεσῳσμένοι) in the middle of a list of the first three main verbs in the passage: "made alive with" (συνεζωοποίησεν), "raised up with" (συνήγειρεν), and "seated with" (συνεκάθισεν). Its insertion after "made alive with" is instructive, since being made alive indicates the initial effects of salvation in a person by the indwelling presence of the Spirit. This Spirit is what enables believers to live or "walk" differently and experience the continued effects of salvation from sin and death. Being saved means living differently in conformity to God's holiness, love, and mission by the power of the Spirit (1:4; 3:16–17; 5:1–2, 17–18).

Importantly, the only active verbs with human subjects serve as part of the contrast between two purpose statements (both introduced by ἵνα): in 2:9, "*in order that* not anyone would boast" (negative), and 2:10d, "*in order that* we would walk/live in them [good works]" (positive). This positive statement of human agency comes only after Paul has established the divine origin and basis of salvation in 2:8a, denied any human origin and agency in 2:8b–9, and affirmed God's role as creator and founder in 2:10a–b.

In 2:10b, the second passive-voice verb is the participle typically translated "being created" (κτισθέντες). Two serious translation problems exist here. The participle translated "created" (from κτίζω) has a broad semantic range and social usage; it and its cognates occur thousands of times in public inscriptions and Greek literature to refer to the "founding" of political-religious institutions: (whole) peoples, colonies, cities, cults, associations, etc. So here, Paul used a social-political idiom that people in Asia Minor would understand. Moreover, typically the preposition ἐπί is translated "for" as if indicating purpose. Purpose, however, is most typically expressed by the prepositions εἰς or πρός. Instead, ἐπί with the dative here indicates "on, on the basis of, because of" good works. Paul argues that "being founded in Christ Jesus" is "on the basis of good deeds that God planned ahead of time." God has planned Jesus's coming to show his followers how to live in good deeds. What this means, then, is that the positive purpose of human agency in 2:10d depends on God's initiative of grace. Believers are to imitate the good works that God pre-planned would be exemplified in the Messiah, Jesus. We are to walk in love and offer ourselves sacrificially in love just as Jesus has done, as God's beloved children (5:1–2).

Fredrick J. Long

The Love between Paul and the Philippian Believers

PHILIPPIANS 1:7

καθώς ἐστιν δίκαιον ἐμοὶ τοῦτο φρονεῖν ὑπὲρ πάντων ὑμῶν, διὰ τὸ ἔχειν με ἐν τῇ καρδίᾳ ὑμᾶς . . .

Paul's letter to the Philippians contains some of the warmest, heartfelt language in all his letters. From beginning to end, Paul shares his affection for these fellow believers. To give just two examples, he calls them "my beloved ones" (ἀγαπητοί μου, 2:12) and commends them for sharing with him in his troubles (4:14). One of the most affectionate moments in the letter comes early on—in Paul's prayer of thanksgiving for these dear friends (1:3–11).

We hear in his prayer that Paul is deeply grateful for their "partnership" (κοινωνία) with him in the gospel (1:5). This is a favorite word of Paul's and refers to the unity that Christians experience with Christ as well as their unity as a community of believers. Because of this profound unity based on the good news, Paul thanks God whenever he remembers the Philippians and prays for them with joy (1:3–4). In what follows, Paul expresses the reason for (the "rightness" of) his experience of deep connection with these Christ followers even though they are separated by many miles and by the walls of Paul's prison cell. He writes in verse 7: διὰ τὸ ἔχειν με ἐν τῇ καρδίᾳ ὑμᾶς. The three-word phrase, διὰ τὸ ἔχειν, is a single collocation signifying cause: "because [someone] has." Since infinitives have their subject as well as any direct object in the accusative case, the two accusatives με and ὑμᾶς are both potential candidates for a subject, with the other acting as the object of the infinitive. So the two possible renderings are: "I have you" or "you have me," with the prepositional phrase "in the heart" referring to whichever is the object ("my" or "your," respectively).

What this means is that Paul's Greek allows for either of these translations:

> "It is right for me to feel this way about you because I have you in my heart."

> "It is right for me to feel this way about you because you have me in your heart."

Now, word order is arranged in favor of the first rendering, since με precedes ὑμᾶς in the sentence. Yet we cannot be definitive on this point, since Greek word order is quite flexible.

What difference does this ambiguity make? First, both readings fit hand in glove with what we hear in the letter about the relationship between Paul and the Philippian church. As we have noticed, he loves them dearly, and they have gone out of their way to show concern for his well-being, not least by sending Epaphroditus to care for him in their place (2:25–30). So either reading would fit Paul's expression of this warm, reciprocal relationship. Second, it is intriguing to wonder whether, after penning this line and rereading the prayer, Paul may have perceived the ambiguity and, rather than somehow "fixing" it, decided that it was the perfect expression of their relationship so valued by both sides.

What difference does this ambiguity make *for us*? Philippians is a letter that provides a window into relationships within the church at their best. While neither Paul nor the Philippian church is perfect (e.g., they need work in the area of unity; 2:1–4; 4:2–3), their relationship is warmhearted and empathetic. When one side is hurting, the other is deeply affected. With God's power (2:12–13), may we, the church, seek out this same kind of joyous responsiveness to one another because *we have each other in our hearts.*

Jeannine K. Brown

Christian Regard for the Other

PHILIPPIANS 2:3–4

³μηδὲν κατ' ἐριθείαν μηδὲ κατὰ κενοδοξίαν, ἀλλὰ τῇ ταπεινοφροσύνῃ ἀλλήλους ἡγούμενοι ὑπερέχοντας ἑαυτῶν, ⁴μὴ τὰ ἑαυτῶν ἕκαστος σκοποῦντες, ἀλλὰ καὶ τὰ ἑτέρων ἕκαστοι.

How many friends do you have on Facebook? Followers on Twitter and Instagram? Connections on LinkedIn? In the digital, social-media age, these kinds of questions can become status markers. Social capital is a powerful commodity. It has always been that way, of course. In the twenty-first century, it revolves around being digitally connected, heard in sound bites, and seen on YouTube clips or Vimeo videos. But even though the media may change, we have much in common with the Roman world of the earliest Christians. Then, too, members of society fiercely competed for attention, status, and "followers." That is precisely why Philippians continues to carry such an important message for the church today, and 2:3–4 in particular (as a prelude to the famous Christ Hymn of 2:6–11) charges Christians with the value of putting others first.

Roman society was agonistic, establishing a culture where one would do virtually *anything* to climb the ladder of success and receive widespread recognition. Rivalry, mockery, and mudslinging were commonplace in any sort of competitive context. That is what makes Paul's counsel to the Philippians all the more remarkable. He makes these key points:

Reject the way of "me vs. you" (ἐριθεία). There is, of course, a good kind of competition where "iron sharpens iron," but Paul is criticizing here the kind of rivalry and strife that stirs up jealousy and fuels spite and revenge. Healthy competition shouldn't focus on "me vs. you" but ought rather to spur everyone on to improve.

Denounce the lust for glory (κενοδοξία). This is a vivid Greek word, literally meaning "vainglory" or "hollow fame." Fame is elusive—you never have enough. You have a hundred followers, you want a thousand. You have a thousand, you want ten thousand. Paul tells them, *Don't fall into that trap. Don't put on a show to draw all eyes to yourself.*

Lift up one another (ἀλλήλους ἡγούμενοι ὑπερέχοντας ἑαυτῶν). Paul does something rather clever here. If Roman life was conceived of as a fight up the ladder of status, Paul tells the Philippians to treat everyone—even those *below* you on the ladder—as if they were *above* (ὑπερέχοντας) you. This is not "doormat" theology, however; it doesn't mean I should devalue myself. Rather, if *everyone* (ἀλλήλων) does this, it subverts the ladder system itself.

Invert the system (ταπεινοφροσύνη). Paul calls for a humble mindset. Literally this word carries the sense of a "lowness perspective." We see a wordplay link with the Christ Hymn when Paul refers to Christ *lowering* himself (ταπεινόω) to take the form of a slave (2:7–8). That is, instead of zealously clawing his way *up* the status ladder, Christ humbly *lowered* himself to lift others up. Henri Nouwen, inspired by Philippians, refers to this as the "downward-mobility" spirituality of Christ.[1]

Turn to the other (σκοποῦντες . . . τὰ ἑτέρων ἕκαστοι). Finally, Paul encourages the Philippians to focus their attention *not* on their own upwardly mobile strategy and activities (τὰ ἑαυτῶν) but on what will seek the benefit of the other.

---

1. See H. Nouwen, *The Selfless Way of Christ: Downward Mobility and the Spiritual Life* (Maryknoll, NY: Orbis, 2007).

Undoubtedly, this would have been a hard message to swallow for many of the Philippians, and it stands as a substantial challenge for us today. What would it mean for us to be visible, present, and attentive to the "nobodies" and conversely invisible and absent to those who could enhance our image and reputation? It sounds crazy, but no crazier than a king who willingly became a slave.

Nijay K. Gupta

Greek and Echoes of Scripture

COLOSSIANS 2:13

Ability to study the New Testament in Greek enables one to overhear echoes of Old Testament Scripture that would otherwise remain undetected if studying the text in translation. Take Colossians 2:13 as an example. Paul writes:

καὶ ὑμᾶς νεκροὺς ὄντας τοῖς παραπτώμασιν καὶ τῇ ἀκροβυστίᾳ τῆς σαρκὸς ὑμῶν, συνεζωοποίησεν ὑμᾶς σὺν αὐτῷ, χαρισάμενος ἡμῖν πάντα τὰ παραπτώματα.

And you, being dead in transgressions and in the foreskin of your flesh, [God] brought to life together with [Christ], having forgiven us of all transgressions.

The Greek phrase I've rendered as "foreskin of your flesh" is translated by virtually all English versions as "uncircumcision of your flesh" (ESV; HCSB; KJV; NAB; NASB; NET; NIV; NRSV). However, their translation obscures the direct connection that this phrase has with the foundational circumcision text of Old Testament Scripture: Genesis 17.

In Genesis 17, God reviews and develops the covenant that he has made with Abraham. For his part, God expands his promise that Abraham will become a great nation; now Abraham will become a "multitude of nations" (vv. 4–6). For Abraham's part, God adds the stipulation of circumcision for every male of the covenant community as a sign (vv. 9–14). "They are to cut off the 'flesh of the foreskin' (MT: בְּשַׂר עָרְלַתְכֶם), the prepuce or fold of skin that covers the head of the male genital organ."[1]

This phrase, "flesh of [your] foreskin," is repeated five times in Genesis 17 in both the Hebrew as well as numerous Greek manuscripts and versions. For our purposes, I provide the Greek Old Testament (LXX) readings because it is almost certainly the version the apostle echoes at Colossians 2:13:

Genesis 17 and the Phrase "Flesh of [Your] Foreskin"

Verse 11:	περιτμηθήσεσθε	τὴν σάρκα τῆς ἀκροβυστίας ὑμῶν
Verse 14:	περιτμηθήσεται	τὴν σάρκα τῆς ἀκροβυστίας αὐτοῦ
Verse 23:	περιέτεμεν	τὴν σάρκα τῆς ἀκροβυστίας αὐτῶν[2]
Verse 24:	περιέτεμεν	τὴν σάρκα τῆς ἀκροβυστίας αὐτοῦ
Verse 25:	περιετμήθη	τὴν σάρκα τῆς ἀκροβυστίας αὐτοῦ

The phrase functions as the direct object of the verb περιτέμνω ("to circumcise") in each instance. In Colossians 2:13, Paul echoes this phrase but reverses the word order (see above). Why?

In a subtle yet brilliant play on words, Paul "refers not primarily to the Colossians' physical uncircumcision, but to their previous *spiritual* uncircumcision—their state of deadness in trespasses and exclusion from God's (new) covenant people."[3] They were not in need of a circumcision that removed only a part of the flesh but of one that cut off the entire "body of flesh" (v. 11)—the Adamic, fallen existence that belonged to this dying age. Just two verses earlier Paul had written that in Christ the Colossians had "already been circumcised [περιτέμνω] with a circumcision not made with hands, consisting in the removal of the body of flesh" (v. 11). This further confirms our interpretation of v. 13.

Old Testament quotations, allusions, and echoes in the New

---

1. Christopher A. Beetham, *Echoes of Scripture in the Letter of Paul to the Colossians*, BibInt 96 (Leiden: Brill, 2008; repr., Atlanta: Society of Biblical Literature, 2010), 183.
2. Following the reading of numerous manuscripts cited in the apparatus of the Larger Cambridge critical edition of the Septuagint.
3. Beetham, *Echoes of Scripture*, 189.

provide a foundation for building a biblical theology of the Christian canon and aid us in understanding how the story of Scripture hangs together as an epic whole. Knowing Greek only further facilitates the construction of this worldview since then we are equipped to detect less explicit yet significant references to the Old Testament that are otherwise obscured in translation. Detection of this particular echo suggests that the apostle understood physical circumcision in the Abrahamic covenant as a signpost to the circumcision of the heart in the new covenant inaugurated in the death of Messiah Jesus (Deut 30:6; cf. Rom 2:28–29; Phil 3:3).

Christopher A. Beetham

Serving Our Master
COLOSSIANS 3:24

τῷ κυρίῳ Χριστῷ δουλεύετε.

Paul's discussion of household responsibilities in Colossians 3:18–4:1 is odd in the context of the letter. First, in a letter that showcases the final and unique authority of Christ (see especially 1:15–20), it is surprising to find Paul now affirming the authority of the male head of the household, who is the husband, father, and master. Second, the way this discussion is introduced is unusual as Paul moves from a call to worship (3:15–17) to the discussion of household relationships. Third, within this discussion the disproportionate space devoted to the exhortation to slaves is noteworthy; only one verse is devoted to every other role within the household (wives, 3:18; husbands, 3:19; children, 3:20; fathers, 3:21; masters, 4:1), but four verses are devoted to slaves (3:22–25). At the center of these verses is the clause τῷ κυρίῳ Χριστῷ δουλεύετε (v. 24). The word δουλεύετε can be taken as an indicative (as in most English versions) or as an imperative (as in most recent commentaries). The imperatival reading is preferable in light of the other imperatival clauses in this section (vv. 18, 19, 20, 21, 22; 4:1) and as a parallel to the imperative in 3:23 ("do it wholeheartedly"). A closer examination of the significance of the call to "serve the Lord Christ" (3:24) will shed light on these three related issues.

First, although Paul appears to be focusing on the authority of the male head of the household, the emphasis is actually placed on the lordship of Christ. In ancient household codes, the adult male was often considered lord of the household. In Paul's discussion of household relationships, however, Paul repeatedly uses the title ὁ κύριος in redirecting attention away from the adult male to Jesus Christ himself (3:18, 20, 22, 23, 24; 4:1). In verse 24 Paul explicitly identifies "Christ" as ὁ κύριος, to whom all members of the household should submit. In an epistle that highlights Jesus as ὁ κύριος (cf. 1:3, 10; 2:6; 3:13, 17; 4:7, 17), this discussion of household relationships emphasizes how the cosmic lordship of Jesus is to be lived out in mundane reality, as symbolized by this setting.

If the lordship of Christ is considered the center of Paul's discussion of household relationships, then the section that precedes (3:15–17) forms an appropriate introduction to this discussion. In 3:17, for example, Paul provides a general call to believers: "Whatever you do [πᾶν ὅ τι ἐὰν ποιῆτε] . . . do everything in the name of the Lord Jesus." This call is repeated at the center of Paul's discussion of household responsibilities: "Whatever you do [ὃ ἐὰν ποιῆτε], do it wholeheartedly, as to the Lord" (v. 23). Paul's discussion of household relationships therefore is an application of his general call to recognize Jesus as the Lord of all.

The connection between the call in v. 17 and the one in v. 23 also explains the emphasis Paul places on the responsibility of the slaves in vv. 22–25. It is easy for modern readers to forget that ὁ κύριος is a relational term, one that is often paired with ὁ δοῦλος. If we confess Jesus Christ as our "Lord," we are acknowledging that we are his "slaves." In an epistle that focuses on the lordship of Christ, Paul now shifts to our responsibilities as Christ's slaves. The lengthy discussion on the responsibilities of slaves in vv. 22–25 then becomes a vehicle for Paul to address the responsibilities of every believer. It is only with this understanding of believers as "slaves" that the repetition of the call in vv. 17 and 23 can be understood: as slaves exist to serve their masters, believers exist to serve their Lord Christ. This would also explain the length of Paul's treatment on slaves.

It is within this wider theological framework that the δουλεύω/δοῦλος word group becomes important in the second half of Colossians. The clause τῷ κυρίῳ Χριστῷ δουλεύετε becomes a call for every believer to act and behave like δοῦλοι Χριστοῦ Ἰησοῦ. This equation is applied explicitly in the final section of Colossians when Epaphras, the founder of the church in Colossae, is identified as δοῦλος Χριστοῦ Ἰησοῦ (4:12); similarly, Tychicus, another prominent Christian leader, is also identified as σύνδουλος ἐν κυρίῳ (v. 7). Though both were free citizens, they were "slaves" of Christ. This metaphoric use of slavery language is confirmed in Paul's introduction of one who literally was a slave; in this instance, instead of identifying Onesimus as δοῦλος, Paul calls him "the faithful and beloved brother" (v. 9). This should have made it clear to the ancient audience that the slavery language was being used primarily as a metaphor to depict the relationship between Jesus and his followers.

As we claim Jesus Christ to be our Lord in hymns and prayers, we need to submit to him as his slaves. We exist for his pleasure, and we live as his instruments. It is only with such recognition that the confession of "Jesus is Lord" can be a meaningful one.

David W. Pao

A Gospel Happening

I THESSALONIANS 1:4–7

⁴εἰδότες, ἀδελφοὶ ἠγαπημένοι ὑπὸ [τοῦ] θεοῦ, τὴν ἐκλογὴν ὑμῶν, ⁵ὅτι τὸ εὐαγγέλιον ἡμῶν οὐκ ἐγενήθη εἰς ὑμᾶς ἐν λόγῳ μόνον ἀλλὰ καὶ ἐν δυνάμει καὶ ἐν πνεύματι ἁγίῳ καὶ [ἐν] πληροφορίᾳ πολλῇ, καθὼς οἴδατε οἷοι ἐγενήθημεν [ἐν] ὑμῖν δι᾽ ὑμᾶς. ⁶καὶ ὑμεῖς μιμηταὶ ἡμῶν ἐγενήθητε καὶ τοῦ κυρίου, δεξάμενοι τὸν λόγον ἐν θλίψει πολλῇ μετὰ χαρᾶς πνεύματος ἁγίου, ⁷ὥστε γενέσθαι ὑμᾶς τύπον πᾶσιν τοῖς πιστεύουσιν ἐν τῇ Μακεδονίᾳ καὶ ἐν τῇ Ἀχαΐᾳ.

In 1 Thessalonians 1–2, there is a stirring description of Paul's arrival (τὴν εἴσοδον ἡμῶν τὴν πρὸς ὑμᾶς, 2:1) in the city and the response to the gospel. These chapters have an unusual concentration of the word for "becoming" (γίνομαι), referring to an event or happening; in the language of the KJV, the word is often translated "it came to pass."

The verb γίνομαι occurs over 660 times in the Greek New Testament; as a common word, it has no intrinsic religious sense, though it is sometimes found in contexts of theological importance (e.g., John 1:3; Rom 1:3; Gal 4:4; Heb 11:3). The semantic range of γίνομαι, "to be, come to pass, happen," overlaps with εἰμί, but γίνομαι implies a change in circumstance: "To possess certain characteristics, with the implication of their having been acquired."[1] The distinction between εἰμί and γίνομαι is made clear in Jesus's remarkable statement, "Before Abraham was [γενέσθαι], I am [εἰμί]" (John 8:58). It is also a natural lexical

---

1. L&N, "γίνομαι," 1:149 (13.3).

choice for the narration of successive events, as in the frequent use of καὶ ἐγένετο, "and it happened," in the Synoptic Gospels.

The "happening" at Thessalonica is described in ten different ways. They can be noted in the order of the text: The gospel *became* (1:5a). It *came* with power, the Holy Spirit, and a full conviction on the part of the preachers. Then again, the preachers *became* (v. 5b). Their conduct was known by the Thessalonians. Finally, the hearers *became* imitators (v. 7). They *became* types for others. The next chapter centers on Paul and the church. Paul's entrance did not *become* empty (2:1). Neither did his preaching *come* with flattering words (v. 5). He *became* gentle toward them (v. 7), and they *became* beloved to him (v. 8). He *became* admirable in their eyes, having led a blameless life (v. 10). They *became* imitators of suffering churches (v. 14). Ten uses of the same verb (γίνομαι, "to become")!

This repetition of γίνομαι refers to a threefold happening in—for want of a better word—a "revival," or perhaps one of our words closer to the authentic New Testament idea of "evangelism." The first is the becoming of the *word*, the power of the gospel proclaimed. Then there is the becoming of the *believers* in Jesus Christ; they are transformed, and their lives give evidence of it. Lastly, there is the becoming of the *messengers*, the heralds of the saving word, who pass the test of character. They all together are essential to this happening.

First in line is the *evangel*—the powerful gospel. The word came with "power and the Holy Spirit" (1:5). Paul's words were accepted "not as the word of men but as what it really is, the word of God, which is at work in you believers" (2:13). To be entrusted with the word of God leaves no room for using the power of words to deceive and to exploit. Paul's denials of unwholesome motives have a staccato effect: no falsehood, no moral impurity, no trickery, no flattery, no cover-ups to manipulate people, no people-pleasing speeches. The only word that stays with believers is the living, abiding word of God.

Second, the *evangelized*—the transformed believers. The Thessalonians turned from idols to serve the living God and became a "model" or "example" for the entire surrounding region. They became witnesses to the gospel, "trumpeting out" the word of the Lord and sharing their newfound faith (1:8).

Third, the *evangelists*—the entrusted heralds. A small pronoun found in 1:5 (οἷοι) is translated in the NIV as "how." The KJV reads "what manner of"; others translate it, "what kind of." There are two ideas conveyed by this pronoun: *who we are* and *what we do.* Paul was keenly aware of preserving the honor of the ministry by living an exemplary life before those he served. He states the heart of being God's servant: "We are approved by God to be entrusted with the gospel" (2:4). He would not separate his *ministry* and his *message* from *himself.* The Thessalonians knew how he behaved among them (2:10), and they followed him: "You became imitators of us and of the Lord" (1:6). The servants of God should become models of the Christian faith, that is, they should serve as a pattern for others to follow. Paul says six times in his letters that his readers should imitate him (1 Cor 4:16; 11:1; Phil 3:17; 4:9; 1 Thess 1:6; 2 Thess 3:7, 9). For that reason, he tells the disciples at Philippi, "Whatever you have learned or received or heard from me, or *seen in me*—put it into practice" (Phil 4:9 NIV).

Bruce Corley

Timothy Shares "Good News" with Paul

I THESSALONIANS 3:6

Ἄρτι δὲ ἐλθόντος Τιμοθέου πρὸς ἡμᾶς ἀφ' ὑμῶν καὶ εὐαγγελισαμένου ἡμῖν τὴν πίστιν καὶ τὴν ἀγάπην ὑμῶν, καὶ ὅτι ἔχετε μνείαν ἡμῶν ἀγαθὴν πάντοτε, ἐπιποθοῦντες ἡμᾶς ἰδεῖν καθάπερ καὶ ἡμεῖς ὑμᾶς.

Paul had a special relationship with the Thessalonian church and with Timothy his young protégé. He explains in his initial letter to the Thessalonians how he came to adore them and could not help baring his soul to them (2:8). Unfortunately, he had to flee from Thessalonica due to persecution and did not have a good chance to say good-bye or give an explanation for his sudden departure. His disappearance undoubtedly unsettled some of the believers, who thought perhaps that Paul was not the person they had held in such high esteem.

His first letter to the Thessalonians bears some marks of the apostle trying to reconnect with these believers and reassure them that he did not willingly abandon them, that he deeply cares for them, and that he hopes that they will respond with the same affection. Though Paul had to leave Thessalonica quickly, he sent Timothy to minister to them to fill the sudden void. It evidently troubled the apostle deeply that his beloved converts might come to question his integrity and the gospel he preached.

Paul comments in this first correspondence how overjoyed

he was when Timothy returned with a good report. The Greek text of 3:6 expresses this emotion in a remarkable way. Paul uses the word εὐαγγελίζομαι in reference to Timothy's positive news (εὐαγγελισαμένου ἡμῖν). This is actually one of Paul's favorite words, and it is apropos in this context because Timothy did indeed share "good news." But you might notice that this verb happens to be central to how Paul talks about *the* good news, the "gospel" of Jesus Christ. The verb εὐαγγελίζομαι occurs about twenty times in Paul's letters and is used almost as a technical reference to the preaching of the gospel of Jesus Christ (e.g., 1 Cor 1:17), with this exception in 1 Thessalonians 3:6. What are the chances that Paul *happens* to be using εὐαγγελίζομαι merely in a mundane way this time?

Obviously in 1 Thessalonians 3:6 Paul is using εὐαγγελίζομαι as a reference to the "good report" of Timothy about the fondness and faith of the Thessalonians toward himself (and Silas and Timothy), but it seems appropriate when reading the Greek text here to add in the "gospeling" nuance of this word in Paul's vocabulary. I imagine Paul pacing back and forth in Athens, nervous and hopeful about Timothy's news. Upon Timothy's return, perhaps by the look Paul sees on his face, I imagine Paul bursting into joyful tears, feeling as if the "good news" of the Thessalonians' shared love, spiritual resilience in persecution, and ongoing loyalty to Christ was an outworking of *the* good news. And here is the clinching fact: this is the only time in all of Paul's letters where he mentions that *he* is the recipient of "good news." This example is a hearty reminder that preachers and Christian leaders are as in need of being "gospel-ed" as anyone else. What a joy and privilege it is when we are ministered to by our own spiritual children and disciples!

Nijay K. Gupta

Chosen unto Salvation

2 THESSALONIANS 2:13–14

¹³Ἡμεῖς δὲ ὀφείλομεν εὐχαριστεῖν τῷ θεῷ πάντοτε περὶ ὑμῶν, ἀδελφοὶ ἠγαπημένοι ὑπὸ κυρίου, ὅτι εἵλατο ὑμᾶς ὁ θεὸς ἀπαρχὴν εἰς σωτηρίαν ἐν ἁγιασμῷ πνεύματος καὶ πίστει ἀληθείας, ¹⁴εἰς ὃ ἐκάλεσεν ὑμᾶς διὰ τοῦ εὐαγγελίου ἡμῶν, εἰς περιποίησιν δόξης τοῦ κυρίου ἡμῶν Ἰησοῦ Χριστοῦ.

After instructing them in 2 Thessalonians 2:1–12 regarding "the coming of our Lord Jesus Christ and our gathering unto him" (see v. 1), Paul offers God thanks yet again for his beloved brothers and sisters in Christ who reside in Thessalonica (2:13; see also 1:3; cf. 1 Thess 1:2; 2:13).[1] Earlier in 2 Thessalonians 1:3, the apostle thanks God for the Thessalonians' growing faith and increasing love; in 2:13 (see text printed above) he expresses thanks to God for having chosen them "unto salvation by [the] sanctification of [the] Spirit and belief in [the] truth." Furthermore, Paul propounds in 2:14 that God called the Thessalonians unto a Spirit-inspired, truth-oriented salvation through the apostles' proclamation of the gospel, leading to a glorious inheritance in the Lord Jesus Christ.

While spiritually spectacular, Paul's thanksgiving to God for the Thessalonians in 2:13–14 is exegetically uncomplicated. There is one text critical issue in 2:13, however, that merits further attention. It is not altogether clear in the manuscript tradi-

---

1. Not a few contemporary scholars wonder if Paul was the author of 2 Thessalonians. I continue to think it more probable than not that he is. This is not the venue, however, to take up the matter.

tion of 2 Thessalonians whether Paul wrote that God chose the Thessalonians believers as "firstfruits" (ἀπαρχήν, as printed above and embraced by the editors of the UBS[5] and the NA[28]) or if the apostle wrote that God chose them "from the beginning" (ἀπ᾽ ἀρχῆς).

As with the other New Testament documents, there would have been no separation between letters of the Greek script in the earliest copies of 2 Thessalonians. Neither would there have been punctuation. It is not too difficult, therefore, to see how both readings might have arisen. (As it happens, in early, extant manuscripts it is not always easy to decipher the difference between a handwritten nu [ν] and a handwritten final sigma [ς].) The question, then, arises and persists—which reading is most likely, and why?

Although one should not blithely or prematurely follow a given editorial team's lead, it does in fact seem more likely that Paul wrote ἀπαρχήν rather than ἀπ᾽ ἀρχῆς. Although ἀπ᾽ ἀρχῆς is strongly supported by a number of generally reliable textual witnesses (including Sinaiticus), the phrase appears nowhere else in Paul. Meanwhile, ἀπαρχή is also a widely-attested reading (including Vaticanus) and occurs six other places in Paul (see Rom 8:23; 11:16; 16:5; 1 Cor 15:20, 23; 16:15; cf. Jas 1:18; Rev 14:4). Taken together, then, the scales tip rather in favor of the reading ἀπαρχήν.

So, what does all of this mean, and what does it matter? When Paul thanks God for choosing the Thessalonian Christians as "firstfruits unto salvation," he is suggesting that they are among the first to entrust themselves to God through the glorious gospel of the Lord Jesus Christ. Additionally, he is indicating that they are harbingers of a coming spiritual harvest. Finally, as firstfruits Paul is maintaining that the Thessalonian converts were set apart by and for God and his good purposes.

To be sure, we contemporary Christians are some distance removed from our Thessalonian forebears. That being said, as we embrace God's love and grace through the gospel and stand firm in it, we can offer winsome witness to others through our words and our ways. All the while, the Lord will encourage and strengthen us for and in "every good deed and word" (2 Thess 2:17).

Todd D. Still

A Trustworthy Saying

I TIMOTHY 1:15–16

¹⁵πιστὸς ὁ λόγος καὶ πάσης ἀποδοχῆς ἄξιος, ὅτι Χριστὸς Ἰησοῦς ἦλθεν εἰς τὸν κόσμον ἁμαρτωλοὺς σῶσαι· ὧν πρῶτός εἰμι ἐγώ, ¹⁶ἀλλὰ διὰ τοῦτο ἠλεήθην, ἵνα ἐν ἐμοὶ πρώτῳ ἐνδείξηται Χριστὸς Ἰησοῦς τὴν ἅπασαν μακροθυμίαν, πρὸς ὑποτύπωσιν τῶν μελλόντων πιστεύειν ἐπ᾽ αὐτῷ εἰς ζωὴν αἰώνιον.

One of the most important steps in the exegetical process is to see the big picture, that is, to visualize the relationship between words and word groups and the flow of the biblical narrative or argument. The person who helped me learn how to do this is my friend and mentor, Gordon Fee. He taught his "Advanced Biblical Exegesis" students how to do structural analysis by learning to produce a "sentence-flow schematic."[1] The purpose of this "is to depict graphically by coordination and by indentation and subordination the relation between words and clauses in a passage."[2]

The process is relatively simple. One begins in the top left-hand corner of the page with the subject and predicate (it is usually desirable to rearrange the Greek word order into the typical English subject-verb-object order if it does not interfere with an author's emphasis or a chiasm). As Fee suggests, the rest of the passage "flows" to the right by lining up coordinate words/phrases (e.g., balanced pairs or direct contrasts) and indenting

1. For full directions on this, see Gordon D. Fee, *New Testament Exegesis: A Handbook for Students and Pastors*, 3rd ed. (Louisville: Westminster John Knox, 2002), 41–58.
2. Ibid., 41–42.

subordinate or modifying words/phrases (e.g., adverbs, prepositional phrases, genitives, adjectives). A key step is to isolate all the "structural signals" (i.e., conjunctions, particles, relative pronouns, and sometimes demonstrative pronouns) because many of the key exegetical decisions are made as we see how words/phrases structurally relate to one another. By doing this schematic, it is easier to visualize how the passage "works" and, especially important for preachers and teachers, it helps identify the key point(s) we need to communicate to others.

A passage that I read often in my parish context as a part of our prayer book's preparation for confession is 1 Timothy 1:15–16. Here is a sentence flow of this text:

ὁ λόγος   πιστὸς
                   καὶ
                   ἄξιος
                   πάσης ἀποδοχῆς
        ὅτι
     Χριστὸς Ἰησοῦς ἦλθεν
                   εἰς τὸν κόσμον
                   σῶσαι ἁμαρτωλοὺς
                   ὧν
                   ἐγώ εἰμι   *πρῶτός*
                   ἀλλὰ
                       ἠλεήθην
                            διὰ τοῦτο
                   ἵνα
                   ἐν ἐμοὶ *πρώτῳ*
                   Χριστὸς Ἰησοῦς **ἐνδείξηται τὴν   μακροθυμίαν**
                                    ἅπασαν
                            πρὸς ὑποτύπωσιν
                                τῶν μελλόντων πιστεύειν
                                        ἐπ᾽ αὐτῷ
                                        εἰς ζωὴν αἰώνιον.

What this analysis illustrates is the key notion *"that* [ὅτι] Christ Jesus came into the world to save sinners." Amongst sinners, however, Paul identifies himself as a primary example of how merciful Christ is. Sandwiched between the two phrases expressing the salvific action of Christ ("Christ Jesus came into the world to save sinners," v. 15b, and "Christ Jesus might display immense patience," v. 16b) is the double "foremost" (πρῶτός; vv. 15c, 16a) example of Paul. He is not taking pride in or exaggerating his status as an example; he is just being honest. If Jesus's mercy extends to one such as him—and remember that Paul was leading the persecution against the Lord and his people at the time when Jesus called him (cf. Acts 9:1–5)—then salvation can come to anyone!

This analysis helps preachers and teachers reinforce the loving nature and extent of God's grace. Paul is helping us to remember that Christ did not come into the world to save good people; Christ came to save "sinners." In a sense, Paul is asking us to imagine the person we might think is beyond God's reach. Who might that be for you? A family member? An annoying neighbor? A rival at work? An enemy? A jihadist? Look at that person from whom you expect the worst and listen to what Paul says about them: Christ Jesus came to save *that* one. This is salvation. This is a trustworthy saying.

Dean Pinter

Set Our Hope on God Who Richly Provides Us with All Riches

1 TIMOTHY 6:17

Τοῖς πλουσίοις ἐν τῷ νῦν αἰῶνι παράγγελλε μὴ ὑψηλοφρονεῖν μηδὲ ἠλπικέναι ἐπὶ πλούτου ἀδηλότητι, ἀλλ᾽ ἐπὶ θεῷ τῷ παρέχοντι ἡμῖν πάντα πλουσίως εἰς ἀπόλαυσιν.

From the ancient Greco-Roman moral philosophers to contemporary preachers, the danger of wealth has been a constant theme in ethical discourse. One finds Paul turning his attention to this issue in his first letter to Timothy, where the focus on wealth in 6:17–18 is highlighted by the repeated use of the πλου-word group: πλουσίοις, πλούτου, πλουσίως, and πλουτεῖν. The rhetorical effect of this series of words cannot be missed, especially when this letter was read aloud by its first reader(s).

Three dangers of wealth are noted in this verse, the first two of which would not have surprised the ancient audience. First, in qualifying material wealth with the phrase ἐν τῷ νῦν αἰῶνι, Paul points to the limited value of worldly possessions. In the financial world, it is a well-known dictum that one should focus on long-term investments rather than short-term ones, since the former usually produce a better yield. Paul does not simply focus on the later years of one's earthly life, but makes reference to the age to come in evaluating the relative worth of one's possessions and accomplishments (cf. v. 19).

Second, Paul points to the uncertainty of material wealth. In qualifying wealth with the adjective ἀδηλότητι, Paul follows the Old Testament wisdom traditions as well as the Greco-Roman philosophers in warning his readers of the deceptive power of wealth. For most people through the ages, acquiring wealth is not an end in itself; rather, the goal is what one can acquire with such wealth. While some would assume that wealth would bring happiness, health, friendship, and respect, many have realized that the mere acquisition of wealth can produce none of these lasting senses of fulfillment. The power of even limited wealth to produce anxiety is well documented by ancient moralists. "The sudden wealth syndrome" noted among lottery winners of our time confirms this phenomenon. These "winners" soon realize that acquiring material wealth normally delivers maximum stress and minimum satisfaction, creating more problems than it solves.

Moving beyond these two points, which were likely familiar to his readers, Paul highlights a more fundamental danger of wealth: the temptation to consider oneself a proud benefactor. Other ancient writers also warned against pride, since for many people wealth could buy them the status of being a "benefactor," that is, a person who was honored because of his or her sponsorship of less wealthy "clients." Here, Paul uses the rare ὑψηλοφρονεῖν, a verb that appears here for the first time in extant Greek literature, highlighting the importance of this warning. To be "haughty" belonged to the rights of wealthy benefactors, but Paul immediately reminds his readers that it is God himself who is the only true benefactor since it is he who "richly provides us with all things for our enjoyment" (v. 17). The greatest danger of wealth is the illusion that one can become a benefactor who competes with God in gaining the respect and honor of one's clients.

This discussion of wealth actually began in an earlier part of the chapter that culminates in 6:10: "The love of money is the root of all kinds of evil." What lies between verses 10 and 17 may appear to be an excursus on the lordship of Christ, but a closer reading reveals that these verses are immediately relevant for the discussion on wealth. In these verses, Paul emphasizes that it is "God, the blessed and only Ruler, the King of kings and Lord of lords" (v. 15), who alone deserves all "honor and might" (v. 16). He is the ultimate benefactor, who gave up his Son, who has died for us and would return as "our Lord" (v. 14). Embedded in these two sections on wealth (6:1–10, 17–19), this affirmation of God as benefactor becomes a necessary corrective for those who assume that wealth can help in establishing one's status as a benefactor.

Paul would, in fact, go on and encourage his readers to be benefactors (vv. 18–19), but these benefactors are to submit to the ultimate benefactor as they focus on the eternal life that is made possible by him who gave up his Son on the cross. Paul's discussion on the danger of wealth is, therefore, not merely an ethical call to be a wise and moral being but a call to worship God and him alone.

David W. Pao

The Gospel, the Cure for Cowardice

2 TIMOTHY 1:7

"Cowardice, alone of all the vices is purely painful—horrible to antici-
pate, horrible to feel, horrible to remember."   *C. S. Lewis*[1]

οὐ γὰρ ἔδωκεν ἡμῖν ὁ θεὸς πνεῦμα δειλίας, ἀλλὰ δυνάμεως καὶ
ἀγάπης καὶ σωφρονισμοῦ.

One of the benefits of learning Greek is the ability to examine
specific nuances of a certain word. In 2 Timothy 1:7 the
noun δειλία is typically translated as "fear" or "timidity." Thus,
Paul is telling Timothy that the Spirit that God has given his people is not a Spirit that produces fear but one which produces power,
love, and a sound mind. This captures the gist of the text, but this
noun δειλία typically has the stronger nuance of "cowardice," especially in the context of battle (note the "good soldier" discussion in
2:3–4). This noun shows up in other ancient texts when soldiers
are instructed to stay at their posts despite the presence of a stronger
enemy or impending defeat. Those who turn and run are described
as demonstrating δειλία, "cowardice." One ancient writer described
cowardice as "a sort of fearful yielding of the soul."[2]

In 2 Timothy Paul has already seen many of his associates
turn away from him in his time of imprisonment (1:15). He tells

---

1. C. S. Lewis, *The Screwtape Letters*, rev. ed. (New York: Macmillan, 1982), 136.
2. Theophrastus (371–287 BC), *Characters* 25. Found in Theophrastus, *Characters.
Herodas: Mimes. Sophron and Other Mime Fragments*, trans. J. Rusten and I. C. Cun-
ningham, LCL 225 (Cambridge, MA: Harvard University Press, 2003), 123.

Timothy he expects better things of him because he remembers his "sincere faith" (1:5). Therefore, Paul exhorts him to courage, reminding him that the Holy Spirit does not inspire cowardice in the hearts of believers. It is the devil who is the source of cowardice. As Proverbs 28:1 says, "The righteous are bold as lions, but the wicked flee when no one pursues."

Cowardice is a natural human response, but it is the truth and power of the gospel which frees us from cowardice and enables true courage. As Paul says in the following verses, this courage comes from the gospel by the power of God because through it death is abolished and life and immortality are brought to life (1:10). This is why Paul (and thus other believers) can suffer and not be ashamed (1:12).

Writing in the first century, close to the time of Paul, the Jewish philosopher Philo described δειλία as "a disease graver than any that affects the body since it destroys the faculties of the soul. Diseases of the body flourish but for a short time, but cowardice is an inbred evil, as closely inherent or more so than any part of the bodily system from the earliest years to extreme old age, unless it is healed by God. For all things are possible to Him."[3] Philo was right: only God can heal this cowardice. What Philo did not know, what the New Testament reveals, is that God heals this disease of the soul through the forgiveness and eternal life made available by the death and resurrection of Jesus Christ.

Ray Van Neste

---

3. Philo, *On the Virtues* 26. Found in *On the Special Laws, Book 4. On the Virtues. On Rewards and Punishments*, trans. F. H. Colson, LCL 341 (Cambridge, MA: Harvard University Press, 1939), 79.

The Importance of Faithful Pastors

TITUS 1:9

ἀντεχόμενον τοῦ κατὰ τὴν διδαχὴν πιστοῦ λόγου, ἵνα δυνατὸς ᾖ καὶ παρακαλεῖν ἐν τῇ διδασκαλίᾳ τῇ ὑγιαινούσῃ καὶ τοὺς ἀντιλέγοντας ἐλέγχειν.

In his letter to Titus, Paul gives instruction on establishing church health among what appear to be fairly new churches. These churches are already afflicted with false teachers, who are "disrupting whole households" with their teaching (1:10–16; 3:9–11). Paul will give significant teaching to counter these false teachers, but he begins with the need for faithful local pastors or elders (1:5–9). When you are reading the Greek text, you can see how often words used to describe these pastors in 1:5–9 are picked up later in the letter. For example, while the pastors' children are not to be rebellious (ἀνυπότακτα, 1:6), the false teachers *are* rebellious (ἀνυπότακτοι, 1:10). The pastors are described as "not pursuing dishonest gain" (μὴ αἰσχροκερδῆ, 1:7), but the false teachers do their work "for the sake of dishonest gain" (αἰσχροῦ κέρδους χάριν, 1:11). The pastors are to be "self-controlled" (σώφρονα, 1:8), and this idea becomes a central description of proper Christian living later as older men and younger men are instructed to be "self-controlled" (σώφρονας, 2:2; σωφρονεῖν, 2:6). The verb used for the older women's work of "urging" younger women to love their husbands and children (σωφρονίζωσιν, 2:4) is also connected to this concept.

Furthermore, the description of the faithful pastors ends with a resounding emphasis on their teaching ministry. In ancient times, as in our day, lists of various things were common. One way ancient writers stressed a certain item in a list was to put that item either at the beginning or end of the list and then to expand on that same item, thus highlighting it. Notice the list of qualities for pastors in 1:5–9. Many are a single adjective or an adjective negated with μὴ. There are a few terse three-word phrases. Then, the final characteristic that takes up all of verse nine—a participial phrase with a ἵνα clause coupled with two infinitives! This characteristic jumps out as having significantly more expansion, indicating that it is a point of particular emphasis. The point here is the teaching ministry of the pastors and its twofold aim: instructing in sound doctrine and refuting false teaching. In fact, this introduces the rest of the letter. The concern about refuting (ἐλέγχειν, 1:9) those who oppose sound doctrine introduces the fact that such opposition will be described in 1:10–16 and 3:9–11 and that Titus must "refute" them (ἔλεγχε, 1:13). The point about exhorting in "sound doctrine" (τῇ διδασκαλίᾳ τῇ ὑγιαινούσῃ, 1:9) introduces 2:1–15 where Paul expounds "sound doctrine" (τῇ ὑγιαινούσῃ διδασκαλίᾳ, 2:1) and the lifestyle that befits it.

Reading the Greek text allows one to see these verbal repetitions revealing the careful structuring of the argument and accentuating the importance placed on pastoral ministry. Crete was well known as a rough, immoral place. For these young churches in Crete to thrive, Paul's first concern is that they have faithful pastors. The godly behavior of these pastors would provide models for the people as they learned to live as Christians. The godly character of Crete's pastors also stood in bold contrast to Crete's false teachers. Even if the believers could not pinpoint the precise error of the false teachers, they should be able to say, "Our pastors don't act this way." Additionally, the importance of the teaching ministry is stressed as pastors are called to both negative and positive ministry: refuting error and teaching truth. Both aspects are still needed for believers to mature and for churches to be healthy today.

Ray Van Neste

Reconciliation and Grace

PHILEMON 16

οὐκέτι ὡς δοῦλον ἀλλὰ ὑπὲρ δοῦλον, ἀδελφὸν ἀγαπητόν, μάλιστα ἐμοί, πόσῳ δὲ μᾶλλον σοὶ καὶ ἐν σαρκὶ καὶ ἐν κυρίῳ.

In our modern global context, slavery is more prevalent than ever with an estimated twenty-seven million slaves worldwide.[1] While this is appalling to contemporary readers, slavery was commonplace in the ancient world. Paul challenges the status quo of his time, proposing a shocking perspective in his letter to Philemon.

Contrasts permeate the Greek language of Philemon 16. The first and most obvious contrast is between δοῦλον and ἀδελφὸν ἀγαπητόν. The master/slave relationship by nature was one of inequality. To receive Onesimus as ἀδελφὸν ἀγαπητόν instead of δοῦλον was to receive him as an equal, a dear brother in Christ, and a friend, just as Philemon would have received Paul (v. 17). This is even more striking when placing δοῦλον with the negating adverb οὐκέτι in juxtaposition to δοῦλον with the positive preposition of excess, ὑπέρ. Both uses of δοῦλον are appositional to αὐτόν in v. 15, and ἀδελφὸν ἀγαπητόν is in epexegetic apposition to ὑπὲρ δοῦλον. Paul is declaring that a change has taken place in the life of Onesimus that will forever transform his relationship with Philemon.

---

1. Kevin Bales, *Disposable People: New Slavery in the Global Economy* (Los Angeles: University of California Press, 2012), xxxiv, note 3.

Two adverbs of comparison are also telling. The adverb μᾶλλον denotes that one thing is greater, higher, or better than another (rather than simply comparing two similar nouns, as with ὡς at the beginning of this verse). The distinction is further amplified by the qualifying interrogative pronoun πόσῳ before μᾶλλον.

Differing indirect objects, ἐμοί and σοί, are presented as the ones receiving the escaped slave as ἀδελφὸν ἀγαπητόν. The second indirect object is surprising. When describing Onesimus as a brother in Christ, the reader expects something like ἐμοί, πόσῳ δὲ μᾶλλον τῇ ἐκκλησίᾳ, distinguishing the benefit that another brother in Christ can bring not only to one person (Paul) but also to the larger body of Christ, the church. Instead, Paul states that the greater benefit is for Philemon.

In addition, Onesimus is of value to Philemon καὶ ἐν σαρκὶ καὶ ἐν κυρίῳ. In this case, the reader would perhaps expect καὶ ἐν σαρκὶ καὶ ἐν πνεύματι, as flesh and spirit often occur together. But Paul brilliantly chooses κυρίῳ, which would have clearly been understood as a designation for Christ as well as for a slave master or lord. We might hear the ancient context more appropriately if translated as "both in the flesh and in the Master." This word choice immediately calls attention to the Master of Christians—a striking and final, culminating contrast in the verse. The language places Philemon and Onesimus on equal ground as believers. There is one Master, the Lord Jesus Christ, and therefore their relationship has changed, even if Onesimus by Roman law remains the slave property of Philemon. Such transformation is reminiscent of Galatians 3:28: "There is neither Jew nor Greek, there is neither slave nor free, there is neither male nor female; for you are all one in Christ Jesus."

Paul is aware of the biblical provision to set free an escaped slave (Deut 23:15–16), while at the same time he has respect for the Roman law that mandates their return. Hence, in Christian love for Philemon and Onesimus Paul writes a compelling letter seeking restoration and grace. Perhaps he hopes for the manumission of Onesimus, but if not, he certainly redefines the relationship between Onesimus and Philemon as one of equality in Christ.

Paula Fontana Qualls

The Divine High Priest

³ᵃὃς ὢν ἀπαύγασμα τῆς δόξης καὶ χαρακτὴρ τῆς ὑποστάσεως αὐτοῦ, ᵇφέρων τε τὰ πάντα τῷ ῥήματι τῆς δυνάμεως αὐτοῦ, ᶜκαθαρισμὸν τῶν ἁμαρτιῶν ποιησάμενος ᵈἐκάθισεν ἐν δεξιᾷ τῆς μεγαλωσύνης ἐν ὑψηλοῖς.

Hebrews 1:3 belongs to one of the most beautiful sentences in the Greek New Testament (1:1–4). While the pile of clause upon clause can seem daunting to the beginning Greek student, this flowing structure contributes to the majestic vision of the Son of God that the preacher (author) of Hebrews ultimately desires. Knowing the Greek will help the reader to appreciate great theological truths. The focus in this essay is on v. 3 and particularly how the participial clauses relate to each other and to the main verb ἐκάθισεν.

There are two common views about the relationship of the participial clauses. First, one could highlight the tenses of the participles. The first two participles in v. 3 are in the present tense: ὢν and φέρων. The following participle is aorist: ποιησάμενος. Often aorist participles describe an action that occurs before the main verb, while present participles refer to an act that occurs simultaneously with the main verb. By using the present participle to introduce the statement that the Son is the "radiance of the glory and the exact imprint of his character," the preacher would be indicating that this status of glory is connected to the Son's exaltation.

Alternatively, one could understand the clauses to indicate a sequential movement from preexistence (v. 3a–b) to incarnation (v. 3c) to exaltation (v. 3d). Additionally, the participles ὤν and φέρων could have a concessive sense so that the author is contrasting the Son's glorious identity and role with his sacrificial act ("although being"; "although bearing"). The sense would be something like this: *Although the Son exists as the glorious representation of the divine, and although he sustains creation, after he gave himself as a purifying sacrifice he then was exalted to God's right hand.* On this reading, the significance of the present-tense participle is not temporality but continuous action. The point of the present-tense participle in this case is not to indicate a condition that occurs at the same time of the main verb ἐκάθισεν. Instead, the present tense highlights the character of the Son and his sustaining role in relationship to creation (v. 2) as continuous activities.

Deciding which option is correct is not easy. Both are grammatically possible and theologically on target. Given the preacher's masterful facility with Greek, it may be that he intended some ambiguity, although I suspect that it is the second option that is the more accurate. Perhaps most importantly, though, is this: the emphasis actually lies in the contrast between the Son's glorious state and his humiliation in an act of atonement. The author claims that the pathway to the Son's exalted and superior name was through suffering. And it is this majestic vision of the Son of God that the preacher expounds upon throughout the rest of his sermon and calls his listeners/readers to emulate.

Jason Maston

Faith's All-Star

HEBREWS 12:1–2

δι' ὑπομονῆς τρέχωμεν τὸν προκείμενον ἡμῖν ἀγῶνα, ²ἀφορῶντες εἰς τὸν τῆς πίστεως ἀρχηγὸν καὶ τελειωτὴν Ἰησοῦν.

How is Jesus being presented in these two verses? Many translations would have us look to Jesus as "the pioneer and perfecter of *our* faith" (NRSV, emphasis added; cf. KJV, ESV, NLT); others lead us to look to Jesus as "the pioneer and perfecter of faith" itself (NIV; so also NASB, CEB). The difference—the presence or absence of a single word in the English ("our")—is significant. Reading with the NRSV, we are led to think of Jesus in terms of what he does for us, the contribution he makes to "our faith" (typically "the faith we exhibit"). Yet following along with the NIV, we are led to think of Jesus as the one who has gone further ahead than anyone else into the territory of faithful action (the "pioneer" or "scout") and as the one whose faith toward God has come to its most complete expression (the "perfecter").

The first thing to notice is that there is no actual word for "our" (e.g., τῆς πίστεως ἡμῶν) in the Greek. This is not in itself decisive, since it is indeed sometimes implied and appropriately supplied. Within Hebrews there is a good example: in 10:22 we read the exhortation, "Let us keep drawing near . . . having sprinkled our hearts from a bad conscience and having washed our body with clean water." In the Greek we find simply "the hearts" and "the body," but the reader would rightly sense that the author is talking about "*our* hearts" and "*our* body," in large part because of the middle voice of the verbs (these are actions we have done *to ourselves*, a reflexive sense of the middle voice being appropriate in this particular context). In that case, the author in 11:40 would be speaking of the hope that the pre-Christian worthies would be made perfect along with us, and this might suggest that what is being perfected in 12:2 is us—*our* faith.

There are two contextual factors, I believe, that have greater weight and thus point away from adding the pronoun. The first is the rhythm and focus of all of 11:1–38, which shows what faith looks like in action, the very faith that the hearers were being called to embody in the midst of their own challenges (see 10:32–39, especially 10:39). The parade of exemplars of faith is not over until we get to the king of the parade, Jesus himself, in 12:2. The second is what the author goes on to say about Jesus in the remainder of 12:2–3, which has everything to do with how he exhibited faith (very much in line with, though *outdoing*, the sterling examples in chapter 11 in terms of despising shame and enduring hardship for the sake of God's reward), and nothing particularly to do with his work in the believer's heart.

It seems likely, therefore, that the author is presenting Jesus as the high-water mark of "faith in action," the ultimate model for us as we seek to follow where he has gone as our forerunner (6:19–20). This is particularly important for disciples who are facing hardship for their faith. These are encouraged to exhibit similarly costly faith (to "run with endurance") both by Jesus's example—which ends in exaltation and honor in God's presence—and by the awareness that Jesus's example of such faith was designed to benefit them, made abundantly clear by this point in the sermon (2:9, 14–15; 9:11–14, 24; 10:12–14). Until we, too, have resisted to the point of shedding blood (12:4), we have not begun to keep faith as Jesus kept faith (cf. 13:12–13).

David A. deSilva

God, Give Us Birth

¹³μηδεὶς πειραζόμενος λεγέτω ὅτι Ἀπὸ θεοῦ πειράζομαι· ὁ γὰρ θεὸς ἀπείραστός ἐστιν κακῶν, πειράζει δὲ αὐτὸς οὐδένα. ¹⁴ἕκαστος δὲ πειράζεται ὑπὸ τῆς ἰδίας ἐπιθυμίας ἐξελκόμενος καὶ δελεαζόμενος· ¹⁵εἶτα ἡ ἐπιθυμία συλλαβοῦσα τίκτει ἁμαρτίαν, ἡ δὲ ἁμαρτία ἀποτελεσθεῖσα ἀποκύει θάνατον. ¹⁶Μὴ πλανᾶσθε, ἀδελφοί μου ἀγαπητοί. ¹⁷πᾶσα δόσις ἀγαθὴ καὶ πᾶν δώρημα τέλειον ἄνωθέν ἐστιν, καταβαῖνον ἀπὸ τοῦ πατρὸς τῶν φώτων, παρ᾽ ᾧ οὐκ ἔνι παραλλαγὴ ἢ τροπῆς ἀποσκίασμα. ¹⁸βουληθεὶς ἀπεκύησεν ἡμᾶς λόγῳ ἀληθείας, εἰς τὸ εἶναι ἡμᾶς ἀπαρχήν τινα τῶν αὐτοῦ κτισμάτων.

In English, there is some limited "gendering" of inanimate objects, such as referring to a ship as "she." But usually in English one uses masculine and feminine genders only to refer to creatures that are phenomenally male and female (certain contemporary discussions of human gender and sexuality aside). This is different from Greek, in which everything has gender. This difference between the languages can make one miss the depth of what is going on in a Greek text.

In James 1:13 the point is made that no one who is undergoing testing should blame God. (The shift in many English translations from "testing" or "trials" in 1:12 to "temptations" in 1:13 is misleading, for 1:13 has the verbal form [πειράζω] of the noun πειρασμός found in 1:12 and is starting a restatement and expansion of 1:2–8.) Of course, such blaming is precisely the human tendency: "God, or someone other than me, made me do it." It starts in Genesis 3:12 ("the woman whom *you* gave to be with me . . ."). In Genesis 22:1, however, it does say, ὁ θεὸς ἐπείραζεν τὸν Ἀβρααμ (LXX; "God tested Abraham"). But by James's time the testing of Abraham in Genesis 22:1 was read through the lens of Job, where Satan tests Job with the (perhaps grudging) permission of God. As a result, James can say, "God tests no one."

"Ah, yes," the implied reader implicitly replies, "but I am experiencing a testing situation." James responds to the unstated question, "You are tested by your own desires." At this point, he wants the reader to realize that their failure in a test is their own fault, not God's (v. 13). Whether one was a Stoic or influenced by the Jewish *yētser* tradition (good impulse/bad impulse), human drives or emotions were viewed as unbridled and thus the root of all vices. The difference among the traditions was the solution they offered: What would control ἐπιθυμία ("desire")? For the Stoic it was reason, λόγος, and for the Jew, Torah. James has a place for both, but he also plays with two other images.

The word ἐπιθυμία is feminine, so James uses its grammatical gender to form a play on words (vv. 14–15). *She* "entices" the person, then gets pregnant by the person, and then gives birth to a daughter, ἁμαρτία, "sin." Now ἁμαρτία grows up and, it is implied, also gets pregnant and gives birth to a son, θάνατος, "death." And, of course, death is the end of the chain. The point is that it is all the person's fault: *they* are enticed by *their* desire; *they* "sleep" with sin; *they* end up with death.

Where is God in all of this? He is not part of the problem at all, but part of the solution. In 1:2–8, if one is having a problem with πειρασμός, one is to ask God, and he will give one another "spouse" than ἐπιθυμία, namely, σοφία ("wisdom"). This draws on the rich Jewish literature about Lady Wisdom. In 1:17, James goes farther. God only gives good and never changes, so he could never be part of the testing situation. He has nothing to do with the desire-sin-death chain. Instead, he deliberately, not accidentally, "chose" (the aorist participle βουληθεὶς indicates that these implied readers are already believers) to give birth to "us" (v. 18). This verb, "gives birth," is the same verb, ἀποκυέω, that is used for "sin" giving birth to death in v. 15. It is a verb only used for a female giving birth, not for a male causing a female to give birth. To underline this lexical fact, a "male" is brought in, λόγος, but not the Stoic λόγος, for James's λόγος is characterized by ἀλήθεια, "truth." This is the good news itself. "We" are, therefore, the first-fruits of creation (humanity as the crown of creation or the new humanity as the crown of the renewed creation).

James has played a game with gendered images. The uncontrolled desires that are in a person ultimately lead to death. But God, who can never give anything but good, reverses the action of desire and sin by, so to speak, taking the female role and deliberately giving birth to the believer so that the believer has new life. Consequently, the believer is the best of the creation that God is bringing into being. And the believer is the best in that he or she is born and not just made.

Peter H. Davids

Advice to Christian Husbands

I PETER 3:7

Οἱ ἄνδρες ὁμοίως συνοικοῦντες κατὰ γνῶσιν, ὡς ἀσθενεστέρῳ σκεύει τῷ γυναικείῳ ἀπονέμοντες τιμήν, ὡς καὶ συγκληρο-νόμοις χάριτος ζωῆς, εἰς τὸ μὴ ἐγκόπτεσθαι τὰς προσευχὰς ὑμῶν.

How are Christian husbands to bear themselves toward their believing wives, and for what reasons? English translations have been far from precise in regard to answering this question. The ESV and NIV are representative:

> Likewise, husbands, [A] live with your wives in an understand-ing way, [B] showing honor to the woman [A'] as the weaker vessel, [B'] since they are heirs with you of the grace of life, so that your prayers may not be hindered. (ESV, letters added)
>
> Husbands, in the same way [A] be considerate as you live with your wives, and [B] treat them with respect [A'] as the weaker partner and [B'] as heirs with you of the gracious gift of life, so that nothing will hinder your prayers. (NIV, letters added)

In both translations, two actions are presented as desirable: (A) showing consideration toward one's wife, and (B) showing honor or respect to one's wife. Further, in both translations, two implicit motives are provided for the second stance: (A') "as [= since she is] the weaker partner" and (B') "as [= since she is] a fellow heir of the gift of life." The structure of the Greek sentence, how-ever, is quite different than either translation suggests:

Οἱ ἄνδρες ὁμοίως,
(Α) συνοικοῦντες κατὰ γνῶσιν
(Α') ὡς ἀσθενεστέρῳ σκεύει τῷ γυναικείῳ,
(Β) ἀπονέμοντες τιμήν
(Β') ὡς καὶ συγκληρονόμοις χάριτος ζωῆς.

Thus, an English translation reflecting the (fairly transparent) structure of the Greek would read: "The husbands in the same way, (A) living together considerately with your wives (A') as with the more fragile, feminine vessel; (B) showing them honor (B') as also fellow heirs of the gift of life, so that your prayers may not be hindered."

The author first introduces a snapshot of a husband's ethical behavior with which Greco-Roman philosophers on the household could agree: the woman's more fragile constitution is not something to be exploited or dominated by the self-seeking man; rather, it calls for restraint and other-centered consideration, a *yielding* of power in the face of fragility rather than the *wielding* of the same. The author then introduces a second snapshot that is distinctive to the marriage between two Christians: the woman's status in God's family as an heir alongside the man calls for honor and respect on the latter's part, something that might surprise the Greco-Roman philosopher. If we read the verse in this way, we will *not* make the mistake of thinking that showing honor to the Christian wife is a magnanimous gesture toward the "weaker vessel." Rather, we will hear that such respect is her due by virtue of what God has made her along with the husband. The identity of husband and wife as "fellow heirs" specifically recalls the sibling relationship into which *all* Christians have entered by virtue of being born into God's family (see 1 Pet 1:22–23; 3:8; 5:9). This introduces a counterdynamic into the relationship: marriage in the ancient world was conceived of as inherently hierarchical, but the relationship of brothers and sisters was not—and *this* is the author's final word on Christian marriage.

The adverb "likewise" (ὁμοίως) beginning this particular instruction calls for some comment. "You husbands, likewise" in regard to what? "Likewise" as the wives (3:1–6), who are told to do "likewise" (3:1) as the slaves (2:18–25), all likewise submitting themselves "to every human institution" and "honoring everyone" (2:13, 17)? The author makes his point clear—I am not to define others' roles in regard to myself or my authority, but to lavish honor and respect upon my fellow heirs.

David A. deSilva

Why We Stray Sexually
2 PETER 2:14

ὀφθαλμοὺς ἔχοντες μεστοὺς μοιχαλίδος καὶ ἀκαταπαύστους ἁμαρτίας, δελεάζοντες ψυχὰς ἀστηρίκτους, καρδίαν γεγυμνασμένην πλεονεξίας ἔχοντες, κατάρας τέκνα.

When Greek texts are translated into English, it often necessitates breaking up long sentences in a way that, unfortunately, may obscure the relationship between the smaller parts of the sentence. Participles often play a major role in organizing a number of phrases into one sentence or unit that demonstrates a closer relationship between them than an English translation may convey. For example, in 2 Peter 2:14 the use of participles throws light on the relevant topics of seduction, adultery, sexual harassment, and sexual abuse within God's people.

Second Peter addresses the topic of spiritual abuse by "false teachers" (ψευδοδιδάσκαλοι), who infiltrate the fellowship (2:1). Their influence is not so much that of official leaders in the church hierarchy but rather of covert influence through spreading their opinions and providing examples of unrestrained immorality (2:2, ἀσελγείαις). In 2:3 their abuse takes the form of exploitation.

"These people" (οὗτοι) are compared in 2:12 to animals who live by instinct and are destined for destruction. A series of participles provides the reason for their destruction in 2:13–14. These participles are sometimes understood and translated as *predicate participles* or *independent participles*: "They are those who. . . ." However, the participles are indisputably linked to a finite verb. Therefore, while these labels may help us to determine the breakdown of our sentence structure in English translation, in the Greek they are adverbial participial phrases that modify φθαρήσονται (2:12, "they will be destroyed"). Together in a parallel construction, they are all present participles that portray the aspect of the actions as unfolding or being in process. Moreover, they are all *causal*, providing reasons for the destruction that will fall upon the false teachers. In addition, they are related to each other and interpret each other rather than forming an atomistic list in which the elements have no relationship to one another.

The first three causal participles in 2:13 provide a context for 2:14: "suffering" (ἀδικούμενοι) the penalty for doing wrong, "considering" (ἡγούμενοι) it a pleasure to carouse, and "indulging" (ἐντρυφῶντες) in their dissipation. These participles set the stage of showing their immoral behavior so that their condemnation has specific causes.

The three causal participles in 2:14 are our focus in this devotion: the concern about sexual immorality, its victims or prey, and at least one of its sources: "having" (ἔχοντες) eyes full of adultery and insatiable for sin, "seducing" (δελεάζοντες) weak souls, and "having" (ἔχοντες) a heart trained in greed. This is the climax of the arrogance and audacity of the infiltrators (2:10), which is punctuated in 2:14 with a predicate-nominative exclamation: "Accursed children!" This is a clear indictment of a sexualized and sensual worldview, which may be equated to sexual addiction.

The relationship of these parallel participles implies that a person can train their heart for greed in a way that will manifest itself in partying, dissipation, adultery, and seduction—that is, this passage identifies a way in which sexual addiction is cultivated. The Bible does not suggest that anyone is entitled to a sexual addiction, or that anyone (such as a spouse) is obligated to enable or satisfy that addiction, or that the "weak souls" are anything but the victims in this context. Rather 2 Peter condemns the way in which a false teacher/perpetrator has trained their heart to do these things and condemns the worldview that supports it. This places the light of the gospel on and against the contemporary practice of pornography and other sexualized aspects of the media that train the heart to lust with greed. Yet more central to the argument of 2 Peter, it warns us against welcoming those who participate in this kind of behavior into our fellowship on their own terms (without clear repentance and a commitment to recovery) or giving our approval to anyone who does these things (cf. Rom 1:32).

Cynthia Long Westfall

Will the Earth Be Destroyed?

2 PETER 3:10

Ἥξει δὲ ἡμέρα κυρίου ὡς κλέπτης, ἐν ᾗ οἱ οὐρανοὶ ῥοιζηδὸν παρελεύσονται, στοιχεῖα δὲ καυσούμενα λυθήσεται καὶ γῆ καὶ τὰ ἐν αὐτῇ ἔργα εὑρεθήσεται. (NA²⁷)

Ἥξει δὲ ἡμέρα κυρίου ὡς κλέπτης ἐν ᾗ οἱ οὐρανοὶ ῥοιζηδὸν παρελεύσονται, στοιχεῖα δὲ καυσούμενα λυθήσεται, καὶ γῆ καὶ τὰ ἐν αὐτῇ ἔργα οὐχ εὑρεθήσεται. (NA²⁸)

Translations differ, and often one must go to the Greek text to understand why. In this case the last words of 2 Peter 3:10 are variously translated: "The earth and everything that is done on it will be disclosed" (NRSV), "the earth and the works that are done on it will be exposed" (ESV), "the earth and everything [done] in it will be laid bare" (NIV 1984 and 2011), "the earth and its works will be burned up" (NASB). The first three translations basically agree in translating εὑρεθήσεται as "laid bare" or "exposed"; the NASB however assumes the authenticity of a later variant, found first in the fifth-century manuscript Alexandrinus and then the Byzantine tradition, κατακαήσεται, "will be burned up." While virtually everyone is convinced that this variant is basically a repetition of the root found earlier in the sentence and then repeated in the following verses, the NA²⁸ (which will probably become the standard for a future series of translations) has done something different with a similar effect. The editors found a "not" in two eighth-century translations, one in Syriac and one in Ethiopic, believed it must have been original, and so inserted it as οὐχ into the Greek text. What does this decision do to the meaning of the text?

In his Anchor Bible commentary Jerome Neyrey pointed out that the teachers the author of 2 Peter is attacking appear to be influenced by Epicureanism.[1] In that philosophy one lived for today's pleasures because there was no future. Life ended, the world itself would dissolve, and there would be no judgment. But in 2 Peter 3 our author argues for a final judgment, first on the basis of the deluge in Genesis 6–9 (vv. 5–7), then on the basis that while God's timing is not ours, his delay is purposeful, and there is no reason to question whether he will judge (vv. 8–9). Finally, we get a description of this judgment in v. 10. In the NA[27] and the first three translations mentioned above, speaking in terms of the normal ancient worldview, God suddenly strips off the heaven (or firmament), destroying the elements (στοιχεῖα in a cosmic context means the heavenly bodies, sun, moon, and stars) and exposing the earth and its deeds to his sight, much as one might cut the top off an anthill to display what was going on underground. Judgment is real and certain. If, on the other hand, the NA[28] is correct, the Epicurean-influenced teachers our author opposes were right—there is no final judgment since all will be destroyed, and so the present really is all that there is to live for.

Traditional text-critical criteria decide strongly in favor of the earth's being "exposed" and judged. But what does this mean for believers? First, it means that one does need to watch text-critical choices, for they can make a theological difference; they are not just for arcane scholarly debate. Second, and more importantly, it means that the whole earth and everything done in the earth, including that which you and I do, will be openly exposed in the end, and we will reap the result, whether in positive reward

1. Jerome Neyrey, *2 Peter, Jude*, AB 37C (New York: Doubleday, 1993), 122–28.

or negative punishment. In the following context, our author is clear: it is the reality of judgment, not present pleasure or human advancement, that should determine our actions (v. 11). Then we will have nothing to fear when the Lord comes as "a thief [in the night]" (v. 10).

Peter H. Davids

God Is Faithful and Just

1 JOHN 1:9

ἐὰν ὁμολογῶμεν τὰς ἁμαρτίας ἡμῶν, πιστός ἐστιν καὶ δίκαιος ἵνα ἀφῇ ἡμῖν τὰς ἁμαρτίας καὶ καθαρίσῃ ἡμᾶς ἀπὸ πάσης ἀδικίας.

God is "faithful and just." This brief statement in the middle of 1 John 1:9 is easy to minimize or even miss in the beauty of the confession of sin and God's forgiveness. And while confession and forgiveness clearly matter, how do the notions of God's faithfulness and justice fit here? To see the connections clearly, we need to begin with sin.

Sin is a major theme in 1 John. While it is repeatedly acknowledged that all people sin (e.g., 1:8, 10), John *both* draws a line between occasional and lifestyle sin (e.g., walking in the darkness, 1:6; 2:11) *and* reminds his hearers and readers that God offers forgiveness and cleansing from sin. But how does one access this forgiveness and cleansing? What is required on the part of the human person? The first clause of v. 9 gives at least one requirement for receiving forgiveness: confession. In line with the Johannine literature specifically and the New Testament more broadly, the confession John has in view is likely public, not private, and thus practiced verbally in the community of believers (without excluding, of course, the importance of private confession of sins).

The next clause states that God is faithful and just, two descriptors that resonate in ears attuned to the Old Testament, ears that have heard the history of God's dealings with his people. In every moment of Israel's unfaithfulness, God responded by being faithful and just. God's faithfulness and justice differ from human parallels because God is faithful and just even when humans are not.

The final clause of 1 John 1:9 is a dependent or subordinate clause in the Greek and begins with ἵνα, which can be translated "in order that" or "so that." The "ἵνα + subjunctive" clause is common in the New Testament and can be employed in a variety of ways. Two common suggestions for the ἵνα clause here are that it is purpose-result or that it is epexegetical. If the clause is purpose-result, then what is being stressed is God's *intention* to forgive and cleanse (the "purpose" element), along with the sure *completion* of God's intention (the "result" element). In other words, God is faithful and just and thus will not fail in forgiving and cleansing.

However, a better choice may be the epexegetical usage, for this use sees the ἵνα clause as explaining a noun or adjective. Put another way, perhaps John is explaining or expounding upon the two adjectives in the preceding clause, πιστός and δίκαιος, "faithful" and "just." God being faithful and just in this situation *looks like* forgiving sins and purifying from unrighteousness. We might even say that here God *demonstrates* faithfulness and justice in this specific way. This is powerful because it confirms what hearers and readers of the Old Testament already know: God's righteousness and justice are not static attributes but active realities that have been, and still are, lived out in his relationship with his people as he works to restore. This is as true in our time and culture as it was in theirs.

Holly Beers

Born from God

I JOHN 4:4–6

⁴ὑμεῖς ἐκ τοῦ θεοῦ ἐστε, τεκνία, καὶ νενικήκατε αὐτούς, ὅτι μείζων ἐστὶν ὁ ἐν ὑμῖν ἢ ὁ ἐν τῷ κόσμῳ. ⁵αὐτοὶ ἐκ τοῦ κόσμου εἰσίν· διὰ τοῦτο ἐκ τοῦ κόσμου λαλοῦσιν καὶ ὁ κόσμος αὐτῶν ἀκούει. ⁶ἡμεῖς ἐκ τοῦ θεοῦ ἐσμεν· ὁ γινώσκων τὸν θεὸν ἀκούει ἡμῶν, ὃς οὐκ ἔστιν ἐκ τοῦ θεοῦ οὐκ ἀκούει ἡμῶν. ἐκ τούτου γινώσκομεν τὸ πνεῦμα τῆς ἀληθείας καὶ τὸ πνεῦμα τῆς πλάνης.

The Johannine literature, including the Epistles and the Fourth Gospel, is famous for being at one and the same time both simple and incredibly profound. The early church described John's writing as shallow enough for a child to wade in while being deep enough for an elephant to swim in.

This is a reflection of John's theological profundity. But it is also true about the style and use of Greek in the Johannine writings. John's Greek is remarkably simple and thus it is the typical starting place for students who are learning to read Koine. Yet this simple Greek, sometimes overly repetitive and uninteresting in style, hides a depth that is worth closer attention.

One such example in the Epistles of John is his use of the preposition ἐκ followed by a genitive phrase. In the short letter of 1 John, ἐκ phrases occur a remarkable thirty-four times. But much more important than the frequency is the core theological truth he ties to these expressions. John uses ἐκ phrases to describe the world in a binary way—every person has their identity, origin, and nature in one of two realms. One realm is God; the other realm is everything not from God.

Thus, we see ἐκ used on the positive side for believers in Christ, who are ἐκ τοῦ θεοῦ, ἐκ τοῦ πατρὸς, ἐξ αὐτοῦ, ἐκ τῆς ἀληθείας, ἐκ τοῦ πνεύματος. On the opposite side, we encounter unbelieving people, who are described as ἐκ τοῦ διαβόλου, ἐκ τοῦ πονηροῦ, ἐκ τοῦ κόσμου, and not ἐκ τῆς ἀληθείας. First John 4:4–6 above contains a concentrated section of these phrases, especially the important ἐκ τοῦ θεοῦ.

In vocabulary lists we are taught that ἐκ plus the genitive should be rendered "out of, out from." Many English translations instead render it with the simple "of," because "out of" would clearly be misleading on occasion (e.g., ἐκ τοῦ κόσμου in v. 5 doesn't translate well as "out of this world!"). Both of these glosses, however, miss the bigger theological point being made: everyone in the world, according to John, can be described as having their metaphysical identity and nature and existence either from God or apart from him. John uses the apparently simple ἐκ to communicate this important theological idea. There is no good English gloss that can render this well—"of" is probably the best, but the meaning is deeper than our translations into English can convey.

These seemingly simple and even tedious ἐκ phrases may be the stuff of first-year Greek on the surface. Yet when examined more closely, they are essential to John's theological program: to paint a picture of the world in stark contrast between God and his people and the world that he loves but that is opposed to him. Though not easy to translate, these ἐκ phrases invite John's readers to consider the very nature of humanity and the world in relation to God.

Jonathan T. Pennington

Fill Up Your Joy Tank
2 JOHN 8

βλέπετε ἑαυτούς, ἵνα μὴ ἀπολέσητε ἃ εἰργάσασθε ἀλλὰ μισθὸν πλήρη ἀπολάβητε.

Watch yourselves, that you do not lose what we have accomplished, but that you may receive a full reward. (NASB, 1995)

Joy is one of humanity's most treasured experiences. Relationships, power, prestige, wealth, entertainment, and indulgences are sought as means to savoring joy. Yet such efforts have no guarantee of filling us up with joy. Here in 2 John 8, we see a key to receiving a full reward. By looking more closely at John's use of the Greek term πληρόω, "to make full," we will see that a full reward includes the treasure of joy.

The key to receiving a full reward is to "keep watch." Already in this short letter, John has described the commands to walk in truth and to walk in love as two sides to one coin (vv. 4–6). Further, he has established the seriousness of not walking in truth and love, describing it as deception and as the antichrist (v. 7). Then in verse 8, John includes the imperative βλέπετε ἑαυτούς, "to watch yourselves," and what will happen if we don't, and what will happen if we do.

In context, "keeping watch" means to hold on to the truth and to walk in love. It means to walk according to Christ's commandments (v. 6), to not be deceived (v. 7), to abide in the teaching of Christ (v. 9), and to not receive false teachings or false teachers (v. 10). John desires to elaborate on the theme, and he hopes to speak to them in person so that their joy may be made full (v. 12).

Here John is echoing what he had learned from Jesus about abiding fully in the truth and how this is the key to joy. He had written in his Gospel that Jesus said, "These things I have spoken to you so that my joy may be in you, and that your joy may be made full" (John 15:11) and "These things I speak in the world so that they may have my joy made full in themselves" (John 17:13). In all three of his epistles, John continues to highlight joy and how that joy may be made full. "These things we write, so that our joy may be made complete" (1 John 1:4; "complete" is πληρόω). "I hope to come to you and speak face to face, so that our joy may be made full" (2 John 12). "I have no greater joy than this, to hear of my children walking in the truth" (3 John 4). All of these verses point to the relationship between the fullness of truth and the fullness of joy.

In 2 John, John strengthens the ties between fullness of truth and fullness of joy by using πληρ- terms twice in proximity. The first is the adjective πλήρης in v. 8 in the subjunctive phrase that they might receive a "full" reward if they keep watch. The second is the perfect passive participle of πληρόω in v. 12, that their joy may be made "full" when John speaks to them. John wants to continue teaching them so that they will remain and grow in the truth, and thus their joy will be made full.

If we do not keep watch, if we do not abide in the truth and walk in love, the result is a great loss. John describes this with the phrase μὴ ἀπολέσητε ἃ εἰργασάμεθα (v. 8). The contrasting connective term ἀλλά introduces the next phrase μισθὸν πλήρη ἀπολάβητε. Being deceived and not walking in love are contrasted with receiving a full reward. John emphasizes and makes this exhortation memorable with his use of poetic alliteration, contrasting the rhyming Greek terms ἀπολέσητε and ἀπολάβητε. Paraphrased, John exhorts, "Watch yourselves, that you do not ruin our work, but that you may receive a full reward."

Just as the psalmist had foreshadowed the victory of the cross (Ps 16:10), so he encapsulated this teaching about how to fill up your joy tank. In God's presence is fullness of joy (v. 11). As we stay on the path, abide in the vine, hold on to the truth, and walk in love we will receive a full reward of joy, in this life as well as in the next.

Susan I. Bubbers

Joyful Prayers
3 JOHN 2

Ἀγαπητέ, περὶ πάντων εὔχομαί σε εὐοδοῦσθαι καὶ ὑγιαίνειν, καθὼς εὐοδοῦταί σου ἡ ψυχή.

Beloved, I pray that in all respects you may prosper and be in good health, just as your soul prospers. (NASB, 1995)

As in 2 John, John continues to highlight the theme of joy in 3 John, the shortest book of the New Testament. The prayer formula in verse 2 follows a form of well-wishing common even in secular letters of that era. Nevertheless, John is not just being conventional; he is sincerely praying for Gaius, whom he loves (v. 1). This verse is an example of what to request and how to maintain a heart of joy as we pray for those whom we love.

John expresses joy in both verses 3 and 4. The γάρ introducing these verses points to how this joy prompts his prayer in verse 2. He is joyful because Gaius has been walking in the truth. In particular, he has lovingly supported faithful ministers of the truth (vv. 5–8). Knowing this about him, John equates this with his soul prospering (v. 2). He prays that in all other ways Gaius may also prosper.

A surface reading in the English translation of verse 2 can lead to misunderstandings about what John is praying and why he is praying; therefore, it is important to carefully consider the Greek, especially the terms εὐοδοῦσθαι and καθώς.

The term sometimes translated "prosper" (NASB 1977 and 1995; cf. KJV) is εὐοδοῦσθαι. It is the present, passive infinitive of εὐοδόω. The ancient root has the sense of "to lead on a good path," the verb likely being related to the noun ὁδός "way, road." The term can have a monetary connotation (1 Cor 16:2) or the connotation of success (Rom 1:10). Here in 3 John 2, John intends a broader meaning. He refers in context to Gaius's overall walk in the truth, and he is praying for him in all respects. Here εὐοδόω is best understood as "to experience and enjoy favorable circumstances."[1] This sense is conveyed variously in translations, such as "all may go well with you" (NIV, RSV, ESV), "in all respects you are making good progress" (MIT), and "all is well with you" (NLT).

This understanding of εὐοδόω keeps us from using this verse as a prooftext for insisting that God must provide all the material prosperity we ask for. Mistaking this verse as a guarantee of financial abundance will lead to disappointment and confusion. God might grant prosperity in monetary form, but this is not what John is praying for. He is praying for Gaius "to experience and enjoy favorable circumstances" as he walks the path of truth.

Are these favorable circumstances somehow contingent upon soul prosperity? The English "just as" (NASB) is ambiguous and could be taken as John saying, "If and when your soul is prospering, I pray that other things will prosper." But no, this is not the meaning of καθώς here. In this verse, καθώς is a connective particle used to introduce a comparative clause, not a conditional clause. The mood of εὐοδόω is determined by context, whether it is conveying the idea of actuality or the idea of potentiality.[2] Here John uses an indicative form of εὐοδόω to convey their actual condition. Gaius's soul is flourishing. And John prays that such flourishing will continue in every way. One commentator's translation captures this as "dear friend, I pray that you may prosper

---

1. L&N, "εὐοδοόμαι," 1:247 (22.47).
2. H. E. Dana and Julius R. Mantey, *A Manual Grammar of the Greek New Testament* (New York: Macmillan, 1955), 276–77.

in every way, and be well in body as I know that you are well in spirit."[3]

This understanding of καθώς keeps us from expecting that walking in the truth guarantees pleasant circumstances in life, and it keeps us from thinking that it is up to us to earn prosperity in other aspects of life by having a good spiritual life. Further, the meaning of ψυχή is not narrowly "soul," as if there is a clear distinction between soul and body. One of John's purposes for writing his epistles is in fact to warn against such gnostic dualism. As with the rest of the verse, the term ψυχή is best understood here in a more comprehensive sense, referring to one's life in general. One commentator's translation captures this as "beloved, in all respects I wish for you to prosper and be healthy, just as your life is going well."[4]

As we pray for others, let us truly rejoice with those who rejoice. Let us be genuinely glad when we hear that life is going well for them. And as we follow John's example of praying for those whom we love, let us not presume upon God, but let us trust him to create paths that are filled with his favor and enjoyable circumstances.

Susan I. Bubbers

3. Stephen S. Smalley, *1, 2, and 3 John*, rev. ed., WBC 51 (Grand Rapids: Zondervan, 2008), 341.
4. Robert W. Yarbrough, *1–3 John*, BECNT (Grand Rapids: Baker, 2008), 365.

Jesus Saved His People from Egypt

JUDE 5

Ability to study the New Testament in Greek gives one access to the latest critical edition of the Greek New Testament—the NA[28]—and to its textual apparatus (located at the bottom of its pages). This apparatus provides cutting-edge information regarding the state of the study of the original text of the Greek New Testament.

With the publication of the NA[28] in 2012, a text-critical decision was made that holds significant theological implications if in fact its reading is original. In Jude 5 the committee replaced the word κύριος with Ἰησοῦς after considering all the available primary evidence and the latest in text-critical methodology:

Ὑπομνῆσαι δὲ ὑμᾶς βούλομαι, εἰδότας ὑμᾶς ἅπαξ πάντα ὅτι Ἰησοῦς λαὸν ἐκ γῆς Αἰγύπτου σώσας τὸ δεύτερον τοὺς μὴ πιστεύσαντας ἀπώλεσεν

But I desire to remind you who at one time knew all these things that Jesus, having saved a people from the land of Egypt, afterward destroyed those who had no faith.

The statement is as awkward as it is stunning. Jesus—as in Jesus of Nazareth—saved a people from Egypt? The text alludes to the exodus event as narrated in the Torah. The statement therefore speaks about something that is historically impossible. Jesus of Nazareth was born well over a thousand years after the exodus event and had nothing to do with the liberation of the Hebrews from Egyptian oppression. Of course, a later scribe knew this, stumbling over this reading, and so changed the subject of the verb from "Jesus" to "Lord": κύριος saved a people from Egypt— that is, YHWH, the God of Israel. (The word κύριος is the Greek term used in the LXX to translate the tetragrammaton in the Hebrew Bible.)

However, the New Testament documents bear witness that the earliest church held the conviction that Jesus shared in the divine identity of the God of Israel. The NA[28] reading suggests that Jude understood Jesus to have had an active role in the deliverance and judgment of Israel in the exodus and wilderness wanderings. The author of Jude wrote Ἰησοῦς not merely or primarily as a reference to the historical figure of Jesus of Nazareth but to that figure *as he shared in the divine identity*. Therefore, on this text-critical reading Jude 5 becomes one of the clearest references in the New Testament to Jesus as the preexistent Lord. (The apostle Paul possibly corroborates this idea in 1 Cor 10:1–4 while alluding to Israel's exodus and wilderness wandering: "They all ate the same spiritual food and drank the same spiritual drink; for they drank from the spiritual rock that accompanied them, and that rock was *Christ*" [vv. 3–4 NIV, emphasis added].)

Scholars will continue to discuss this text-critical decision. My point here is not to contribute to that debate but to highlight that knowing Greek and having some ability to navigate the NA[28] textual apparatus opens yet another entire world of exploration and study of the New Testament. Text-critical decisions don't normally hold such import as this particular example—most involve minor issues and readings—but in this case the implications are staggering, contentious, and exciting.

Most English translations won't reflect this significant decision for some years to come.[1] But students of the Greek New

---

1. Though the ESV and NET chose the translation "Jesus" some years before the publication of NA[28], based on the information available in the apparatus of the NA[27].

Testament are privy to the latest scholarly decisions regarding the state of the original text. Knowing Greek means one can read that Jesus saved—and judged—a people from Egypt. That same Lord is the Lord of the church today, who saves and judges with power and ought to be regarded with fear, trembling, and worship.

Christopher A. Beetham

"I'm Still Here"—Jesus

ἰδοὺ ἔστηκα ἐπὶ τὴν θύραν καὶ κρούω· ἐάν τις ἀκούσῃ τῆς φωνῆς μου καὶ ἀνοίξῃ τὴν θύραν, εἰσελεύσομαι πρὸς αὐτὸν καὶ δειπνήσω μετ' αὐτοῦ καὶ αὐτὸς μετ' ἐμοῦ.

Although knowing New Testament Greek encourages Christian faithfulness in countless ways, our knowledge doesn't automatically keep us from sinning. In spite of knowing Greek, we still give in to temptation and sin. And when the sin ruts run deep, you may find yourself asking, "Is Jesus finished with me?" or "Am I a lost cause?" This is especially true for those battling addiction. The accusation and condemnation can be spiritually crippling. Revelation 3:20 speaks powerfully and hopefully into our lives at this point.

Sadly, many Christians have misread (better "underread") Revelation 3:20. I've seen tracts from a leading American evangelist that apply this verse to unbelievers by suggesting that Christ is knocking on their heart's door, ready to enter and begin a new relationship if they will just open the door (i.e., accept Christ). While evangelism is a biblical teaching, this particular text was originally addressed to Christians, and something extremely valuable is lost when we misread the verse.

Revelation 3:20 occurs in the letter to the Laodicean church, a self-sufficient congregation that was seemingly unaware of their spiritual bankruptcy. Drawing on the local setting, Jesus describes this lukewarm bunch as "wretched, pitiful, poor, blind and naked" (v. 17) before reminding them that his rebuke and discipline flow from his love for them. He then calls them to "be earnest [or "committed"] and repent" (v. 19).

Knowing the Greek of v. 20 makes Jesus's promise even more significant. The interjection ἰδού functions almost like another command, shouting us awake to Jesus's ongoing presence: "Here I am!" (NIV) or "Listen!" (HCSB, NRSV, NET) or "Look!" (NLT). Jesus then tells this church that he "stands" (ἕστηκα, the perfect, active, indicative form of ἵστημι) at the door and "knocks" (present, active indicative, κρούω). The verbal aspect of these two terms helps us grasp Jesus's promise.

In Revelation, ἵστημι occurs in the indicative mood as a perfect (3:20; 8:2; 12:4), pluperfect (7:11), aorist (8:3; 11:11; 12:18; 18:17), and future (18:15); the author also uses the perfect participle (5:6; 7:1, 9; 10:5, 8; 11:4; 14:1; 15:2; 18:10; 19:17; and 20:12). This suggests that the author had options, and that his choice of the perfect tense in 3:20 carries significance. The perfect tense (or tense-form) is imperfective in aspect with a spatial value of heightened proximity.[1] The present-tense form κρούω also emphasizes imperfective aspect with a spatial value of proximity. Using the well-known illustration of a reporter and the parade, both the present and the perfect portray the reporter as walking in the parade (rather than viewing it from a helicopter), seeing the action up close. In short, the author is intentional about highlighting the ever-presentness of Christ's invitation. Even for "wretched, pitiful, poor, blind, and naked" believers, Christ hasn't abandoned them. He is still waiting on us to wake up and repent (i.e., open the door to renewed fellowship).

The rest of v. 20 reinforces the personal nature of Christ's invitation. The use of the third-class condition (ἐάν + subjunctive in the protasis and any tense/mood in the apodosis) in this context likely puts the focus back on the exhortations that precede

---

1. Constantine R. Campbell, *Basics of Verbal Aspect in Biblical Greek* (Grand Rapids: Zondervan, 2008), 103–4.

it: "Be earnest and repent! Listen!" The future term δειπνήσω ("dine") has rich socio-historical implications and functions here like a promise. The rich array of personal pronouns ("I" stand and knock, "my" voice, "I" will enter, with "him," "he" with "me") reinforces the intimacy of the promised reunion.

Is Jesus finished with you? Are you a lost cause? No! Jesus is there, waiting on you to turn to him in your brokenness and waiting to be the solution to your brokenness. It's your move.

J. Scott Duvall

Worship the Revealing and Speaking God!
REVELATION 19:10

καὶ ἔπεσα ἔμπροσθεν τῶν ποδῶν αὐτοῦ προσκυνῆσαι αὐτῷ. καὶ λέγει μοι, Ὅρα μή· σύνδουλός σού εἰμι καὶ τῶν ἀδελφῶν σου τῶν ἐχόντων τὴν μαρτυρίαν Ἰησοῦ· τῷ θεῷ προσκύνησον. ἡ γὰρ μαρτυρία Ἰησοῦ ἐστιν τὸ πνεῦμα τῆς προφητείας.

Revelation 19 opens with a crescendo of "hallelujahs" from the great multitude in heaven, the twenty-four elders and the four living creatures, celebrating God's final judgment of the great prostitute (vv. 1–4) and anticipating the wedding of the Lamb, for whom his bride has made herself ready (vv. 6–8). Then the angel tells John to write, "Blessed are those who are invited to the wedding supper of the Lamb!" before adding, "These are the true words of God" (v. 9 NIV).

John responds by falling at the angel's feet to worship him. Immediately the angel responds, "Don't do that! I am a fellow servant with you and with your brothers and sisters who hold to the testimony of Jesus. Worship God!" (19:10a NIV; cf. 22:9). John's improper reaction to the angel (ἔπεσα and προσκυνῆσαι, both aorists) provides the background against which the angel's response shines brightly (λέγει, ὅρα μή, εἰμί, ἐχόντων—all in the present tense). In addition, τῷ θεῷ (dative of direct object) is placed before the verb προσκύνησον to stress that God alone is worthy of worship. (How helpful would it be if our every act of misplaced worship received a "Don't do that! Worship God!" response from any unworthy recipient?) As it does here, normally the verb προσκυνέω takes a dative of direct object when true deity is in view but an accusative of direct object when referring to false deity.[1] One would also perhaps expect the present tense for προσκυνέω ("worship") until we note that every time this verb occurs in the imperative mood in the New Testament, it also occurs in the aorist tense (Heb 1:6; Rev 14:7; 19:10; 22:9).

But the angel's follow-up explanation is of special interest. He begins by identifying himself as a σύνδουλός σού . . . καὶ τῶν ἀδελφῶν σου ("fellow servant with you . . . and with your brothers and sisters"), using the compound σύνδουλος (cf. 6:11 and 22:9) followed by a genitive of association (first σού) and a genitive of relationship (second σού). John and his fellow believers are identified as those who hold to the testimony of Jesus (τῶν ἐχόντων τὴν μαρτυρίαν Ἰησοῦ), in which Ἰησοῦ is likely an objective genitive because the testimony is something they "have" (ἐχόντων; i.e., "testimony about Jesus"). Elsewhere God's people have or hold to the testimony about Jesus (6:9; 11:7; 12:11, 17; 17:6; 20:4; and John only in 1:2, 9). That said, the possibility of a plenary genitive cannot be ruled out entirely—the overcomers have or keep the testimony both by and about Jesus (cf. Rev 1:1: Ἀποκάλυψις Ἰησοῦ Χριστοῦ, "the revelation from/about Jesus Christ").

The angel continues: ἡ γὰρ μαρτυρία Ἰησοῦ ἐστιν τὸ πνεῦμα τῆς προφητείας ("for the witness about Jesus is the same as that spoken by the Spirit in this prophecy"). The predicate nominative τὸ πνεῦμα is taken by most translations to refer to "essence" or "heart," but the NIV (rightly in my view) opts for the Holy Spirit. In Revelation, the Holy Spirit's role is closely linked to prophecy (e.g., the seven messages; 22:6), and he is always called "Spirit" rather than "Holy Spirit." It is the Holy Spirit who produced τῆς προφητείας ("the prophecy"), where τῆς serves a deictic or

---

1. Cf. Daniel B. Wallace, *Greek Grammar Beyond the Basics* (Grand Rapids: Zondervan, 1996), 172.

"pointing" function that normally has a demonstrative force— "this prophecy" (i.e., the book of Revelation).[2] God alone deserves worship, since God the Spirit (rather than an angel) is the ultimate source of the prophetic message. The parallel episode in 22:8–11 also implies that God alone deserves worship because he is the sovereign author of the prophetic message communicated in Revelation.

J. Scott Duvall

---

2. Wallace, *Greek Grammar Beyond the Basics*, 221.

Jesus Is the One Who Is Coming!

REVELATION 22:20

Λέγει ὁ μαρτυρῶν ταῦτα, Ναί, ἔρχομαι ταχύ. Ἀμήν, ἔρχου, κύριε Ἰησοῦ.

In 22:20, Revelation ends with the climactic assertion that Jesus is the one who is the witness to everything that is found in this last book of the canon. He states, "Yes, I am coming soon!" And the response is "Amen, come Lord Jesus." Revelation 22:20 occurs dramatically at the end of the book. It not only has a strategic location, but it connects Jesus with a dominant theme throughout the book: *Jesus* is "the one who is coming." We call this the *parousia* of Jesus Christ, which is a reference to his second coming, but in Revelation it is also a clear claim of divinity.

We first see a reference to "one who is coming" in 1:4: ὁ ἐρχόμενος (from ἔρχομαι, a present, middle, nominative, masculine, singular participle). However, it is not clear at this point in the book of Revelation that this is a reference to Jesus Christ. In fact, vv. 4–5 speak of "Jesus Christ," "the seven spirits who are before his throne," *and* "the one who is and was and is coming."

We can recognize "the one who is and was and is coming" as three descriptions of God, and at this point in the discourse the person so described is distinct from Jesus Christ. Throughout the discourse of Revelation, we will see that John repeats this distinctive pattern as a formula that explicitly refers to God, then he varies the pattern to refer to the beast as an antitype to God. Yet finally he associates the third element of the formula, ἔρχομαι, with Jesus Christ multiple times in a way that forms an unmistakable allusion to the three-part formula.

In Revelation 1:8, the formula is immediately restated and again associated with God: the one who is, and was, and is coming (ὁ ὢν καὶ ὁ ἦν καὶ ὁ ἐρχόμενος) is the Lord God, the Alpha and the Omega, and the Almighty. In 4:8, it is reiterated that "the Lord God Almighty" is the one "who was, and is, and is coming" (ὁ ἦν καὶ ὁ ὢν καὶ ὁ ἐρχόμενος). In 11:17 and 16:5 God is worshiped with the first two elements of the formula as ὁ ὢν καὶ ὁ ἦν ("the one who is and who was").

However, the beast, who represents all that is opposed to God, is referred to twice in 17:8 as the one who "was and is not" (ἦν καὶ οὐκ ἔστιν). The beast that John saw "was and is not and is about to ascend" (ἦν καὶ οὐκ ἔστιν καὶ μέλλει ἀναβαίνειν) and "it was and is not and is coming" (ἦν καὶ οὐκ ἔστιν καὶ παρέσται). In 17:11 the beast is simply referred to as "the one who was and is not" (ἦν καὶ οὐκ ἔστιν). Though these references include several interesting variations of the pattern, it is still recognizable as a wordplay on the formula for God. It indicates that the beast, together with the false prophet and the dragon, parodies God.

When the new heavens and earth are created, God declares, "I am the Alpha and Omega, the Beginning and the End" (21:6). This reminds the reader of God's titles in 4:8, so that when they again appear in 22:12, the associations are clear.

But then in Revelation 22, there are multiple connections that show that Jesus is the one who is coming, with the titles that have earlier been given to God. In the letters to the seven churches Jesus had said, "I am coming soon" twice (ἔρχομαι [. . .] ταχύ; 2:16, 3:11). However, in 22:7 the Lord, the God who inspires the prophets says, "Look, I am coming soon!" (ἔρχομαι ταχύ). This phrase explicitly links up with the formula in 1:4, 8, and 4:8. Then, in 22:12 the one who is coming (ἔρχομαι ταχύ) is "the

Alpha and the Omega, the First and the Last, the Beginning and
End" in v. 13. Jesus identifies himself as the one who sent the
angel with this testimony (v. 16); in turn, the Spirit, the bride,
and all those who hear invite the thirsty to "come" (v. 17).

Therefore, when Jesus clearly says that *he* is the "one who is
coming" (ἔρχομαι ταχύ) in 22:20, it dramatically connects him
to the formula and titles used for God throughout the book of
Revelation. This includes who he was, and who he is, and how he
is distinctive from and set in contrast with the forces that oppose
God. The style and wordplay dramatically and artistically kindle
our passion for Christ's return, provoke us to worship him as
depicted in the throne-room scenes, and equip us to face life's
narratives in the past, present, and future with faith.

Cynthia Long Westfall

Contributors

Holly Beers (PhD, London School of Theology) is Assistant Professor of Religious Studies, Westmont College in Santa Barbara, California. She is author of *The Followers of Jesus as the "Servant": Luke's Model from Isaiah for the Disciples in Luke-Acts* (T&T Clark, 2015) and "Servant of Yahweh" in *Dictionary of Jesus and the Gospels*, 2nd ed. (InterVarsity Press, 2013).

Christopher A. Beetham (PhD, Wheaton College) is Senior Editor, Biblical Languages, Textbooks, and Reference Tools at Zondervan Academic in Grand Rapids, Michigan. He is author of *Echoes of Scripture in the Letter of Paul to the Colossians*, BibInt 96 (Leiden: Brill, 2008; repr., Atlanta: SBL, 2010) and *Colossians and Philemon*, Knowing the Bible (Crossway, 2015).

Jeannine K. Brown (PhD, Luther Seminary) is Professor of New Testament, Bethel Seminary in San Diego, California. She is author of *Matthew*, Teach the Text Commentary Series (Baker, 2015), coeditor of *Dictionary of Jesus and the Gospels*, 2nd ed. (InterVarsity Press, 2013) and *Scripture as Communication: Introducing Biblical Hermeneutics* (Baker, 2007).

Susan I. Bubbers (PhD, London School of Theology) is Dean at The Center for Anglican Theology in Orlando, Florida. She is author of *A Scriptural Theology of Eucharistic Blessings* (T&T Clark, 2013) and *Pet Prayers* (Creation House, 2005).

Bruce Corley (ThD, Southwestern Baptist Theological Seminary) is Senior Fellow at the B. H. Carroll Theological Institute in Arlington, Texas. He is author of *Biblical Hermeneutics* (Broadman & Holman, 2002) and *Colloquy on New Testament Studies* (Mercer, 1983).

Lorin L. Cranford (ThD, Southwestern Baptist Theological Seminary) is retired Professor of Greek and New Testament, living in San Angelo, Texas. He is author of *Learning Biblical Koine Greek*, 4th ed. (C&L, 2002), "Throwing your Margaritas to the Pigs: A Rhetorical Reading of Matthew 7:6" in *Gemeinschaft der Kirchen und gesellschaftliche Verantwortung* (Lit Verlag, 2004), and "Revelation, Doctrine of" in *Encyclopedia of Early Christianity*, 2nd ed. (Garland, 1999).

Peter H. Davids (PhD, University of Manchester) is Director of Clergy Formation, Personal Ordinariate of the Chair of St Peter in Houston, Texas. He is author of *A Theology of James, Peter, and Jude* (Zondervan, 2014), *The Letters of 2 Peter and Jude* (Eerdmans, 2006), *II Peter and Jude: A Handbook on the Greek Text* (Baylor, 2011), *The First Epistle of Peter* (Eerdmans, 1990), and *The Epistle of James* (Eerdmans, 1982).

David A. deSilva (PhD, Emory University), is Trustees' Distinguished Professor of New Testament and Greek, Ashland Theological Seminary in Ashland, Ohio. He is author of *Seeing Things John's Way: The Rhetoric of Revelation* (Westminster John Knox, 2009), *An Introduction to the New Testament: Contexts, Methods, and Ministry Formation* (InterVarsity Press, 2004), *Introducing the Apocrypha* (Baker, 2002) and *Day of Atonement: A Novel of the Maccabean Revolt* (Kregel, 2015).

J. Scott Duvall (PhD, Southwestern Baptist Theological Seminary) is J. C. and Mae Fuller Professor of New Testament and Chair, Department of Biblical Studies, Ouachita Baptist University in Arkadelphia, Arkansas. He is author of *Revelation*, Teach the Text Commentary Series (Baker, 2014) and *Grasping God's Word*, 3rd ed. (Zondervan, 2012).

Nijay K. Gupta (PhD, University of Durham) is Associate Professor of New Testament, Portland Seminary in Portland, Oregon.

He is author of *1–2 Thessalonians* (Wipf & Stock, 2016) and *Colossians* (Smyth & Helwys, 2013).

Paul N. Jackson (PhD, Southwestern Baptist Theological Seminary) is Professor of Biblical Studies at Union University in Jackson, Tennessee. He is author of *An Investigation of* Koimaomai *in the New Testament: The Concept of Eschatological Sleep* (Mellen, 1996), "Background Studies and New Testament Interpretation" in *New Testament Criticism & Interpretation* (Broadman & Holman, 2001), and general editor of *Devotions on the Greek New Testament: Reflections to Inspire and Instruct, Volume 2* (Zondervan, 2017).

Fredrick J. Long (PhD, Marquette University) is Professor of New Testament, Director of Greek Instruction at Asbury Theological Seminary in Wilmore, Kentucky. He is author of *In Step with God's Word: Interpreting the New Testament with God's People* (GlossaHouse, 2017), *Koine Greek Grammar: A Beginning-Intermediate Exegetical and Pragmatic Handbook* (GlossaHouse, 2015) and *2 Corinthians: A Handbook on the Greek Text* (Baylor, 2015).

Jason Maston (PhD, Durham University) is Assistant Professor of Theology at Houston Baptist University in Houston, Texas. He is author of *Divine and Human Agency in Second Temple Judaism and Paul: A Comparative Approach* (Mohr Siebeck, 2010), and coeditor of *Paul and the Apocalyptic Imagination* (Fortress, 2016) and *Reading Romans in Context: Paul and Second Temple Judaism* (Zondervan, 2015).

Susan Mathew (PhD, Durham University) is Lecturer in New Testament at Faith Theological Seminary, Manakala, Kerala, India. She is author of *Women in the Greetings of Rom 16.1–16: A Study of Mutuality and Women's Ministry in the Letter to the Romans* (T&T Clark, 2013).

David R. McCabe (PhD, University of Edinburgh) is Associate Professor of New Testament and Greek at Bethel College in Mishawaka, Indiana. He is author of *How to Kill Things with Words: Ananias and Sapphira under the Prophetic Speech-Act of Divine Judgment (Acts 4.32–5.11)* (T&T Clark, 2011).

David W. Pao (PhD, Harvard University) is Professor of New Testament and Chair of the New Testament Department at Trinity Evangelical Divinity School in Deerfield, Illinois. He is author of *Colossians and Philemon*, Zondervan Exegetical Commentary on the New Testament (Zondervan, 2012), *Thanksgiving: An Investigation of a Pauline Theme* (InterVarsity Press, 2002), and *Acts and the Isaianic New Exodus* (Mohr Siebeck, 2000), and coeditor of *Ascent into Heaven: New Explorations of Luke's Narrative Hinge* (Fortress, 2016), and *Early Christian Voices* (Brill, 2003).

Jonathan T. Pennington (PhD, University of St. Andrews) is Associate Professor of New Testament Interpretation and Director of Research Doctoral Studies at Southern Seminary in Louisville, Kentucky. He is author of *The Sermon on the Mount and Human Flourishing: A Theological Commentary* (Baker, 2017), *Reading the Gospels Wisely* (Baker, 2012), and *Heaven and Earth in the Gospel of Matthew* (Brill, 2007).

Dean Pinter (PhD, Durham University) is Rector, St. Aidan Anglican Church in Moose Jaw, Saskatchewan, Canada. He is author of "Josephus and Romans 13:1–14" in *Reading Romans in Context: Paul and Second Temple Judaism* (Zondervan, 2015) and "The Gospel of Luke and the Roman Empire" in *Jesus is Lord, Caesar is Not: Evaluating Empire in New Testament Studies* (InterVarsity Press, 2013).

Paula Fontana Qualls (PhD, Southern Seminary) is Professor of Religion at Gardner-Webb University in Boiling Springs, North Carolina. She is author of "Mark 11:15–18: A Prophetic Challenge" in *Review and Expositor* (1996) and coauthor of "Isaiah in Ephesians" in *Review and Expositor* (1996).

Rodney Reeves (PhD, Southwestern Baptist Theological Seminary) is Dean and Redford Professor of Biblical Studies at Southwest Baptist University in Bolivar, Missouri. He is author of *Matthew*, The Story of God Bible Commentary (Zondervan, 2017), coauthor of *Rediscovering Paul*, 2nd ed. (InterVarsity Press, 2017), and coauthor of *Rediscovering Jesus* (InterVarsity Press, 2015).

Elizabeth E. Shively (PhD, Emory University) is Lecturer in New Testament Studies at St. Mary's College, University of St. Andrews in Fife, Scotland. She is author of *Apocalyptic Imagination in the Gospel of Mark: The Literary and Theological Role of Mark 3:22–30* (de Gruyter, 2012) and coeditor of *Communication, Pedagogy, and the Gospel of Mark* (SBL, 2016).

Todd D. Still (PhD, University of Glasgow) is Professor of Christian Scripture at George W. Truett Seminary, Baylor University in Waco, Texas. He is coauthor of *Thinking through Paul* (Zondervan, 2014), author of *Philippians & Philemon* (Smyth & Helwys, 2011), and coeditor of *The Lightfoot Legacy Set*, 3 vols. (InterVarsity Press, 2015–17).

Anthony C. Thiselton (PhD, Sheffield; DD, Durham), is Emeritus Professor Canon at the University of Nottingham in Nottingham, England. He is author of *The First Epistle to the Corinthians*, NIGTC (Eerdmans, 2000), *Systematic Theology* (Eerdmans, 2015), and *The Thiselton Companion to Christian Theology* (Eerdmans, 2015).

Ray Van Neste (PhD, University of Aberdeen) is Professor of Biblical Studies at Union University in Jackson, Tennessee. He is coeditor of *REF500: How the Greatest Revival Since Pentecost Continues to Shape the World Today* (Broadman & Holman, 2017), coeditor of *New Testament Theology in Light of the Church's Mission: Essays in Honor of I. Howard Marshall* (Paternoster/Wipf

& Stock, 2011), and coeditor of *Forgotten Songs: Reclaiming the Psalms for Christian Worship* (Broadman & Holman, 2012).

Steve Walton (PhD, University of Sheffield) is Professor in New Testament at St Mary's University in Twickenham, London. He is author of *Leadership and Lifestyle: The Portrait of Paul in the Miletus Speech and 1 Thessalonians* (Cambridge University Press, 2000) and coauthor of *Exploring the New Testament: A Guide to the Gospels and Acts,* 2nd ed. (InterVarsity Press, 2011).

Cynthia Long Westfall (PhD, University of Sheffield) is Associate Professor of New Testament at McMaster Divinity College in Hamilton, Ontario, Canada. She is author of *Paul and Gender* (Baker, 2016), *A Discourse Analysis of the Structure of Hebrews* (T&T Clark, 2006), and coeditor of *The Bible and Social Justice* (Pickwick, 2015).

Scripture Index

Subject Index

Brackets [ ] indicate places where the indexed concept is present, though the exact word may not be used.

Greek Word, Phrase, and Idiom Index

ἀπολέσητε [*aor subj* ἀπόλλυμι] lose, 148

ἀπολλυμένοις [*pr mid ptc* ἀπολλύμι] perishing, 70

ἀπολύω destroy, 26

ἀποκόπτω chop off, 31

ἀνακεκαλυμμένῳ [*pf mid ptc* ἀνακαλύπτω] unveiled, 76

ἀποκυέω gives birth, 133

ἀπονέμοντες [*pr ptc* ἀπομένω] showing, 135

ἄρτος bread, 56

ἀσεβής impious, 59

ἀσθένεια weakness, 79, 85

ἀσθενεστέρῳ more fragile, 135

ἀσθενής weak, 59

βαπτίζοντες [*pr ptc* βαπτίζω] baptizing, 53

βασιλεία kingdom, 20

βλέπετε [*pr impv* βλέπω] Watch! 147

βουληθεὶς [*aor pass ptc* βούλομαι] chose, 133

γάρ for, 30, 31, 32, 68, 70, 78, 79, 87, 90, 150, 160

γέγραπται [*pf pass* γράφω] has been written, 33, 34, 68

γενέσθαι [*aor inf* γίνομαι] was, 105

γενηθήτω [*aor pass impv* γίνομαι] be done, 20

γίνομαι a happening, 105, 106

γράφω write, 34

δειλία cowardice, 119, 120

δειπνήσω [*fut* δειπνέω] will dine, 158

δελεάζοντες [*pr ptc* δελεάζω] seducing, 138

διὰ τὸ ἔχειν because (someone) has, 94

διάβολος devil, 146

(τῇ) διδασκαλίᾳ
(τῇ) ὑγιαινούσῃ (in) sound doctrine, 122

διδάσκοντες [*pr ptc* διδάσκω] teaching, 53

ἐπιστρέψῃ [*aor subj* ἐπιστρέφω] turns, 75

ἐριθεία rivalry, strife, 97

ἔρχομαι come, 162, 163

ἔρχομαι ταχύ I am coming soon, 163, 164

ἔσεσθε [*fut mid* εἰμί] shall be, 53, 55

ἐσταυρωμένον [*pf pass ptc* σταυρόω] crucified, 71

ἐστε σεσῳσμένοι [*pf periph* εἰμί + σῴζω] been saved, 88, 91

ἕστηκα [*pf* ἵστημι] stands, 157

ἕτερος different kind, 83

εὐαγγελίζεται preaches, 82

εὐαγγελίζηται [*pr subj* εὐαγγελίζομαι] might preach, 82

εὐαγγελίζομαι good report, 109

εὐλογητός blessed, 72

εὐοδοῦσθαι [*pr inf* εὐοδόω] to lead on a good path, 150, 151

εὐρεθήσεται [*aor pass* εὑρίσκω] laid bare, 140

εὐχαριστέω thankful, 72

ἔχετε [*pr impv* ἔχω] have, 32

ἐχθρός enemy, 59

ἔχοντες, οντων [*pr ptc* ἔχω] having, 138, 159, 160

ζωή life, 135

ἡγούμενοι [*pr ptc* ἡγέομαι] consider, 138

ἡγούμενοι
ὑπερέχοντας [*pr ptc* ἡγέομαι, ὑπερέχω] consider better, 97

ἤκουσας [*aor* ἀκούω] heard, 48

ἦν καὶ οὐκ ἔστιν [the beast] one who was and is not, 163

ἦν καὶ οὐκ ἔστιν
καὶ μέλλει
ἀναβαίνειν [the beast] the one who was and is not and about to ascend, 163

ἦν καὶ οὐκ ἔστιν
καὶ παρέσται [the beast] the one who was and is not and is coming, 163

σκηνή tent of meeting, divine glory, 80

σκηνόω lived, 80

σκόλοψ thorn, 78

σκοποῦντες [pr ptc σκοπέω] turn to the other, 97

σκεύει τῷ
γυναικείῳ (with the) feminine vessel, 135

σοφία wisdom, 132

σπαράσσω convulse, 26

στίγματα marks, 85

συγκληρονόμος fellow heir, 135

σύνδουλος fellow slave, 104, 160

συνεζωοποίησεν [aor συζωοποιέω] made alive with, 91

συνεκάθισεν [aor συγκαθίζω] seated with, 91

συνήγειρεν [aor συνεγείρω] raised up with, 91

συνοικοῦντες [pr ptc σύνοικέω] living together, 135

συσχηματίζεσθε [pr impv συσχηματίζω] conform to, 64

σῳζομένοις [pr pass ptc σῴζω] being saved, 70

σῴζω save, 18

σῶμα
πνευματικόν body of the Spirit, 47

σῶμα ψυχικόν ordinary body, 47

σωφρονίζωσιν [subj σωφρονίζω] train, 122

σώφρων self-controlled, 121

ταπεινοφροσύνη humility, 97

ταπεινόω lower oneself, 97

ταρασσέσθω [pr impv of ταράσσω] be troubled, 51

τελώνης tax collector, 24

τετάρακται [pf mid of ταράσσω] horrified, 50

Τί ἡμῖν καὶ σοί; What do you have to do with us? 26

τιμή honor, 135

τράχηλον neck, 30

τροφή food, 55

ὑψηλοφρονεῖν [pr inf ὑψηλοφρονέω] to be haughty, 117

φέρων [pr ptc φέρω] sustains, 127, 128
φθαρήσονται [fut pass φθείρω] will be destroyed, 138
φιμώθητι [aor pass impv φιμόω] Be silent! 26
φωνέω cry out, 26
φωνή voice, 50

χάρις grace, gift 79, 88, 91, 135
χρόνος time, 52
χριστός Christ, Messiah, 102, 104
χωλόν lame, 28, 31

ψευδοδιδάσκαλος false teacher, 137
ψυχή life, 152

ὤν [pr ptc εἰμί] exists, 127, 128
ὤφθη [aor pass ὁράω] appeared, 85

Devotions on the Greek New Testament

52 Reflections to Inspire and Instruct

J. Scott Duvall and Verlyn Verbrugge, General Editors

Devotions on the Greek New Testament contains 52 devotions — based on a careful reading and study of the Greek New Testament — written by some of the top Greek scholars of today. Contributors include Scot McKnight, Daniel B. Wallace, Craig L. Blomberg, Mark Strauss, and William D. Mounce, among others.

Devotions on the Greek New Testament can be used as a weekly devotional or as a supplemental resource throughout a semester or sequence of courses. The main point each devotion offers comes from a careful reading of the passage in the Greek New Testament, not from the English Bible. These authors use a variety of exegetical approaches in their devotions: grammatical, lexical, rhetorical, sociohistorical, linguistic, etc. Each devotion closes with a practical application.

Available in stores and online!

Keep Your Greek

Strategies for Busy People

Constantine R. Campbell

Seminarians spend countless hours mastering biblical languages and learning how the knowledge of them illuminates the reading, understanding, and application of Scripture. But while excellent language acquisition resources abound, few really teach students how to maintain their use of Greek for the long term. Consequently, as pastors and other former Greek students find that under the pressures of work, ministry, preaching, and life, their hard-earned Greek skills begin to disappear.

Con Campbell has been counseling one-time Greek students for years, teaching them how to keep their language facility for the benefit of those to whom they minister and teach. He shows how following the right principles makes it possible for many to retain—and in some cases regain—their Greek language skills.

Pastors will find *Keep Your Greek* an encouraging and practical guide to strengthening their Greek abilities so that they can make linguistic insights a regular part of their study and teaching. Current students will learn how to build skills that will serve them well once they complete their formal language instruction.

Available in stores and online!

Biblical Greek: A Compact Guide

William D. Mounce

Biblical Greek: A Compact Guide offers Greek students a one-stop guide for the grammar, morphology, and vocabulary of biblical Greek in a handy size. This resource follows the organization and format familiar to the hundreds of thousands of students who have used *Basics of Biblical Greek Grammar* in their first-year Greek courses, but it is also usable by students who learned with a different grammar. By limiting its discussion to the "nuts and bolts," Greek language students working on translation and exegesis will more quickly and easily find the relevant grammatical refreshers.

Students can, for example, check on the range of meaning for a particular word or make sure they remember how aorist participles function in a sentence. The paradigms, word lists, and basic discussions in *Biblical Greek: A Compact Guide* point students in the right direction and allow them to focus on more advanced Greek study.

Biblical Greek: A Compact Guide will become a valuable addition to the reference library of seminary students and pastors.

Available in stores and online!